...Come what may

TRIBUTES

Melvin L. Cheatham, M. D.
Diplomat, American Board of Neurological Surgery; Fellow,
American College of Surgeons

Come What May is a compelling story of what God can do with two people who are willing to commit their lives totally in His service. This true story is compelling, challenging, inspirational and it is a living example of the great truth that "life becomes full, when you begin to give it away."

Daniel L. Tipton
Doctor of Ministry; General Superintendent, Churches of Christ in
Christian Union

Come What May is a warm, captivating account of the life and ministry of two dedicated servants of God, Don and Twana Hawk. The author, Betty Hockett, presents the story of Don and Twana Hawk from the days of their courtship to the moment God calls Don to his eternal reward. Even then Twana's ongoing passion for God's call upon her life carries this biographical account forward to this current day.

Those who have known members of the Hawk family personally will be reluctant to stop reading. Those who have never known this family will not want to lay the book aside either as they encounter multiplied heartwarming examples of what a committed missionary calling can mean and produce.

For personal reading pleasure, for missions prayer groups, for those going on mission field work teams, especially to Honduras, as missions class collateral reading or for those contemplating a call to missionary careers, this book will be valuable.

A special thanks goes to the author for writing so well a worthy and appropriate account of the lives and ministries of Don and Twana Hawk. All who read this book will be enriched by it.

Doug Ross
President, Evangelical Christian Publishers Association

This is an incredible account of imaginative faith, daring action, and faithful submission to God. It proves that God can use anyone who will trust him—and it demonstrates that our investments in world missions can bring incredible dividends. This amazing story reminds us that God will always provide—*Come What May*!

Hector Newman

Missionary with Mission to the Americas, Tegucigalpa, Honduras

While reading the book I found myself laughing and crying very often. It is one of the most fascinating stories I have ever read of courageous missionaries, couple and family, with a profound commitment to serve the Lord. Each page brings to me great memories as a former student of El Sembrador and as a friend of the Hawk family. I believe this book will be of great encouragement and challenge at the same time to anyone who has chosen to be a Lord's servant.

Saul Gómez Diaz

Pastor and Past President, Honduran Holiness Church; President, Regional Committee of United Bible Society for the Americas

In this book the reader will find the life story and experiences of a man who took God seriously and answered His call to the mission field. Regardless of obstacles that crossed his path, he kept "looking to the invisible" leaving footprints worthy of being followed.

Don and Twana Hawk did not waver in their vision of taking hope to the Honduran youth by means of the redeeming message of the Gospel preached in the classrooms, shops, fields, and in everyday life!

Besides riveting the reader's attention throughout the biography, [the author's] style and content will be a great source of inspiration.

Tom Dunbar

Field Director, World Gospel Mission, Honduras

It is exciting to be a first-hand observer of what God has done through the humble obedience and perseverance of a family that "left all to follow Jesus." In *Come What May* Betty Hockett has also made the reader a first-hand observer, having captured the heartbeat of this family and the school they founded in rural Honduras as it has impacted the nation.

Joseph P. Luce

Chairman, World Gospel Mission Board; former owner Blue Bird Body Company

The story of Don and Twana Hawk's answer of God's call to ministry in Honduras is legendary. They truly gave themselves and what they had to answer His call and to do His bidding. This account of how they were used to establish a beachhead in a foreign land for the evangelism of the youth of Honduras is truly a remarkable story and example of walking by faith. Their faith is still contagious as others continue to answer that call and give themselves to this ministry. Escuela El Sembrador Donald Hawk has impacted the culture of Honduras dramatically.

David C. Le Shana
President Emeritus, George Fox University
Missionary mindedness is not enough! We need to become missionary hearted as well! We need to feel missions as well as think missions! Betty Hockett enlarges our compassion for missions as she tells the amazing story of the Hawk family in Honduras. It is a story of God's faithfulness, a story of answered prayer, and the story of a family's long obedience in serving God. I encourage you to read this well-written account of the work of World Gospel Mission.

Charles Mylander
General Superintendent, Friends Church Southwest
Come What May has suspense, action, laughter, tears, and human drama all wrapped up in real-life missionary biography. Fascinating, yet easy to read, this book you could gladly read to your children or grandchildren (pretending that you were doing it just for them and not for yourself). They will love it, and so will you.

Richard Sartwell
Senior Pastor, Newberg (Oregon) Friends Church
Most Americans, even those who have some general appreciation for the value of missions, haven't the slightest idea what actually goes on in the day-to-day conduct of that enterprise. Betty Hockett lets us see how exciting and inspiring, as well as dangerous and difficult—and just plain human—missions can be. Through the story of the Donald and Twana Hawk family and the farm in Honduras for underprivileged boys called El Sembrador, we learn how the call of God planted in a human heart can over the decades work powerful changes in lives and land. I feel blessed for knowing this story, and I thank God for what He has done through this mission.

Patricia H. Rushford
Speaker, Writer of non-fiction and fiction, including Jennie McGrady series and Helen Bradley series
Come What May is a diary, a story, an adventure, and an accounting of people with a heart for God. The powerful missionary account shares details of the lives of people with a commitment to Christ and Christian service that most only dream of. I was struck most by the faithfulness of the workers and felt a compelling in my own spirit to develop more of a serving heart.

Nancy Hesch
Editor and Publisher, Christian Library Journal

Reading Betty Hockett's *Come What May,* I found myself laughing, crying, and spiritually challenged over the saga of the Hawk family and their farm school for boys in Honduras. The love of the Hawks for one another, their children, and the boys they served shines through Hockett's writing. I read the entire book in one sitting, and found myself encouraged to do better what God has called me to do.

Almon D. White
Past Editor for George Fox Press; Former Christian Booksellers Association Director; Chairman, Board of Trustees, Houston Graduate School of Theology

Betty Hockett has managed without becoming tedious to weave together many details concerning God's call of the Hawk family to mission work in Honduras. The down-to-earth life and the total commitment of Don and Twana Hawk become an inspiration to young and old alike.

Anyone who might read *Come What May* will leave it with the realization that God can and does use those who will commit their life to Him and do whatever it is that He asks of them.

Deborah Hedstrom
Writer, Researcher, Teacher

Come What May throws away the pith helmet and other missionary stereotypes. It replaces them with real, struggling, seeking-to-please-Christ people, Don and Twana Hawk, who decide God is asking them to trade their American [farm] for a Central American jungle. The results plunge the reader into the excitement, danger, and political turbulence of Honduras. Through discouragements, successes, and yes and no answers to prayer, the Hawks cling to one thing—following Jesus Christ, come what may!

Bruce Hicks
General Superintendent, Mid-America Yearly Meeting of Friends

No doubt many accounts of God's wonderful workings never get published. I am glad this one did. I found *Come What May* to be a moving story of the setbacks and successes as Don and Twana Hawk endeavored to reach the lost in Honduras for Christ through the sowing of seeds—in the earth and in the hearts of the people. *Come What May* is a real-life missionary drama filled with tears of joy and tears of sorrow. Through it all, Don and Twana trusted God and gave Him the glory. I am thankful that Betty Hockett has put this remarkable story in print.

Rebecca Thomas Ankeny, Ph.D.
Professor, Writing/Literature, George Fox University
Come What May, the biography of Don and Twana Hawk by Betty M. Hockett, will challenge young people and adults to listen to God and obey God's call. The Hawks show what can be accomplished by ordinary people absolutely committed to obeying God—they can change the world. Betty Hockett's descriptions of Honduras and detail about the Hawks' lives help the reader understand the challenges they faced and their love for the Hondurans and the work.

John F. Sills
General Superintendent, The Evangelical Church
You will have a hard time putting down *Come What May*. This fast-paced account of one family's journey of obedience across nearly fifty years in Honduras will rivet your attention. What Don and Twana undertook under the leadership of God is astonishing. The missionary farm school they built from the roots up has wide respect across Central America. It is no surprise that their own children have returned to El Sembrador as missionaries, also with World Gospel Mission. Give yourself a couple of evenings for some exciting, God-honoring, inspirational reading!

Rev. Joseph T. Duvall
Senior Pastor, Heritage Memorial Church
From Don and Twana Hawk's initial call into missions until today, they have proven to be faithful to their call to reach the people of Honduras. Just as Livingstone was to the Africans and Brainerd was to the American Indians, so the Hawks are to the Hondurans. This book is a "must read" for anyone who has a vision for world evangelization!

by
Betty M. Hockett

Don and Twana Hawk's courage and obedience

to God transform

a Honduran jungle into El Sembrador,

a farm school for underprivileged boys.

COME WHAT MAY

International Standard Book Number 0-913342-89-0

Library of Congress Catalog Card Number: 98-73586

Printed in the United States of America
by Barclay Press, Newberg, Oregon 97132
Cover by Donna Allison
Design and composition by Barclay Press

In memory of Donald Frederick Hawk

and

In honor of Twana Jean Baker Hawk

Whose obedience, courage, and steadfastness added much to the

kingdom of God on earth and in heaven.

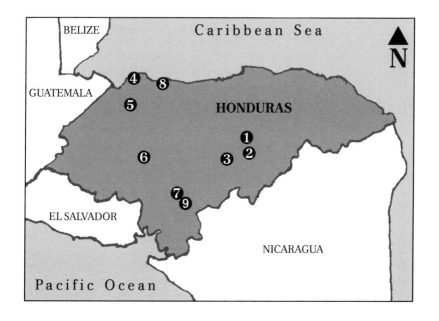

❶	Catacamas
❷	El Sembrador
❸	Juticalpa
❹	Puerto Cortés
❺	San Pedro Sula
❻	Siguatepeque
❼	Tegucigalpa
❽	Tela
❾	Zamarano

TABLE OF CONTENTS

INTRODUCTION xiii

IN THE BEGINNING xv

JUNE 1971 1

1946 – 1954 7

1954 – 1960 77

1960 – 1974 129

1974 – 1993 181

ALBUM 223

FINALLY 240

INTRODUCTION

The story of Don and Twana Hawk and El Sembrador is one that cries out to be told. It is one of the truly great stories of modern-day missionary service.

The vision and commitment of Don and Twana Hawk are certainly extraordinary. Their lives will challenge the reader to a deeper commitment to Christ and stronger desire to be involved in kingdom work.

The exciting aspect of this story is that it is still being lived out. While you read this exciting book, Honduran boys are being trained and educated at El Sembrador with a powerful Christian emphasis.

Now that Don and Twana have laid down the mantle of leadership, many others, including their own children, have picked up the mantle, and the ministry moves forward.

Writer Betty Hockett has done an outstanding job of capturing this amazing story and putting it in a very readable form.

Dr. Thomas H. Hermiz
President
World Gospel Mission

IN THE BEGINNING

When I first heard snippets of El Sembrador's history, saw pictures, and met the Hawk family, my writer's mind at once fell into step with the story. Later, in God's providence and at the invitation of the Hawk family, He gave me the honor and privilege to merge the details of this history into one volume. My gratefulness to God and all others concerned poured out daily as I researched, wrote, and rewrote.

Old Honduras Field Minutes, Field Reports, and, most of all, the Hawk correspondence and articles brought the facts of this story back to life. Scores of people relived their memories through interviews. I thank the Lord for this background material, though the abundance made the sifting and sorting process difficult.

Because space in these pages cannot hold them all, exciting and wonderful details must remain in their original state. Kind people read this manuscript and approved it, but I take responsibility for anything left out purposefully or inadvertently. If I mistakenly omitted your name on the following list of people to whom I am indebted, please accept my apologies:

• **Twana Hawk**, who lived this story in real time and again in writing time; the main starter for the book, and my friend who generously gave her time, friendship, and hospitality, all the while showing great patience for this asker of many questions.

• **My husband, Gene**, who walked alongside, literally and figuratively, even as I gathered information in Honduras.

• **My family and many friends** who put up with my excited chatter about the project and uplifted me with their prayers. I do not live or write in an ivory tower.

• **Sharon Hawk**, superb translator, organizer, and traveling companion. In our humble opinion we made a great interview team.

• **The Hawk children**, their spouses and offspring, who graciously let me probe into their lives, and who gave suggestions and encouragement.

• **Hondurans**, whose names may or may not appear in the story, but who greatly influenced the writing:
Jorge Pinto, a good friend and pastor, who made numerous appointments for us in Tegucigalpa and then joyfully and skillfully drove us to each one; Ricardo Gonzalez; David and Ela Castro; José Hernandez; Virgilio Barahona Lagos; José (Joche) Hernandez; Carlos Enrique Moradel; José Barahona; Miguel Escobar; Arcides Lemus; Natanael Padilla; Roberto Acosta; Belsa Nuñez; José Ricardo Hernandez; José Ventura Escobar; Ramon Mejia; Gumercindo Escobar; Rafael Leonardo Callejas, former president of Honduras; Neli and Adolfo Elvir; Dr. and Mrs. Manuel Figueroa; Hector Newman; Hirnaldo and Marta Molina; Guillermo Jimenez; Saul Gómez; Alejandro Eroza; Luis Oseguera; Raul Pereira; Nicolas Turcio; Carlos Espinoza; Rigoberto Romano; Ramon Enriques; Arturo Donaire; Betty Padilla; Rolando Alvarez; Jochito Hernandez; Linda Flores; Jorge Pacheco; Francisco and Vilma Castro; doña Eloisa de Moradel; Alfredo Moradel; Oscar Hernandez; Rodolfo Figueroa; Juan Bautista Calix; Chepe Santos; Aldens Galindo; Jarler Galindo; Professor Jimenez; Santos Fino; mothers: Dora Hernandez, Sofia, Mari; Edgardo Zapata; doña Tina; Roque Caranza; Luis Escoto; Esperanza Fuentes; Alejandro and Martita Mejia.

• **To those who knew El Sembrador years before I did**, and who willingly remembered and told me what they knew: Marge Brown, who obeyed the Lord and taped testimonies of several former students, traveled to El Sembrador to "help Twana with the book," not knowing I also would be there, and then translated for me during more interviews; Chloe Schneider; Lydia Echlin Warta; Beulah Burgess; George and Marian Hotrum; Hollis Abbott; Doris Sorenson; Bob Smith; Paul Kleman; Don and Eunice Coffman; Lois Henry; Paul Eberhard; Jim and Sheryl Cameron; Larry and Angie Overholt; Tom and Ellen Dunbar; Judy Crist; Mark Dunbar; Liva Keller; Dennis and Marie Hawk; Bill Ware; Charles and Roxie Holbrook; Lillian Harper; Bud Leeth; Don Humble; Grover and Roberta Blankenship; Harvey Bennett; Tim Rickel; Dr. Thomas Hermiz, president of World Gospel Mission; Leona Powell; Billy and Elladean Harrell; Joe Luce; Nellie Thum; Burnis Bushong; Bob and Kathy Owen; Pat and Shirley Hiatt; Art and Doris Vesper; Mel and Sara Eberhard.

Betty M. Hockett
June 1998

JUNE 1971

"Well, Twana, we've had problems here at El Sembrador before," said Donald Hawk to his wife. "We trusted the Lord then and He always helped us, so we'll trust Him now too." He tossed his cap onto the table as Twana filled his coffee cup.

"Did you hear something new when you were in town just now?" she asked.

"Yes. The campesinos (comp-a-SEE-nos) have invaded more land nearby, and they say they're going to take eight hundred manzanas from us."

"But that would be more than half our acreage. We wouldn't have enough land left for the farm to support the school. Or enough pasture for our cattle, either."

"And part of the land they want is where the ditch is for the new power plant."

Don took a big swallow of coffee. "I need to hurry so I can tell the boys the latest."

"Mel just drove by on the tractor. He'll want to know too."

Three Hawk sons, Ted, Tom, Terry, and one daughter-in-law, Joanne, along with Mel and Sara Eberhard completed the missionary staff working with Don and Twana at El Sembrador. Missionaries and their Honduran farm workers all felt the same unsettledness that had started a few weeks before.

This new situation sprouted like a weed, threatening El Sembrador, the two-thousand-acre mission farm school for underprivileged boys in the Olancho district of Honduras. Many poor Honduran farmers looking for a handout grew bold when local as well as outside authorities excited them into action. They organized into a group known as the campesinos and invaded good farmland in several areas.

Because the government owned all the land in Honduras, common practice allowed needful farmers to take over land not used for education, support of a family, research, or protection of natural resources. This time, however, promoters urged the campesinos to take any productive land. "It's rightfully ours," they declared unashamedly.

In April 1948, Don and Twana Hawk had their first view of the farm later named El Sembrador: one acre cleared, 799 acres tangled with thick jungle growth. This young couple from Ohio saw years beyond the sight that day. Instead of carbon (car-BONE) with thorns that reached out to grab and scratch and trees bigger around than any they had seen before, they pictured productive fields and gardens. Their minds placed a herd of well-bred cattle and dairy cows in flourishing pastures. Amongst the birds' whistles and trills, Don and Twana imagined the cheerful noise of lively Honduran boys who otherwise would have no chance at education and perhaps little opportunity to hear about God's love for everyone.

To all this God had called them.

Now, twenty-three years later, the boys chattering in the background, Don gulped the last mouthful of coffee. He grabbed his cap and said on the way out, "I'm sure there's a lot of land in Honduras that hasn't been developed, and for the good of the country it ought to be. I wish the agitators would help the campesinos get those places instead of encouraging them to take over the cultivated land."

Twana turned back to her kitchen duties, slicing bread still faintly warm from the oven. *Trouble never picks a convenient time. There's a whole group of visitors coming in a few days for the new power plant dedication on the twenty-sixth. Then Ted and Joanne's baby is due next month, and we're trying to get ready to go on furlough right after that.*

She smiled at the thought of a third grandchild, the second to arrive in Honduras. Plans for their only daughter's wedding in August also surfaced into Twana's thinking. The campesinos and their threats momentarily sank out of mind.

Before long, though, the present difficulties once more left no space for soon-to-come joys.

"I had hoped this whole thing would blow over, but it doesn't look like it's going to," Don said a few days later. "Ted, you and I and our lawyer had better go to Tegucigalpa (Tay-goo-see-GAL-pah) tomorrow to see the president-elect and the U.S. ambassador. Maybe the newspaper director too. I've asked don (dohn) Luis Oseguera (Loo-EES Osee-GER-a) to go along. He's a good friend, and it'll help to have his business-man's viewpoint in our favor."

Late the next night they returned to El Sembrador. "All the men we talked to thought the farm ought to stay in our hands," Don told Twana. "So now we'll see what happens."

June rains began and with them the time to plant rice and corn. Workers finished the fields between the main house and the Talgua (TAHL-gwa) River. After that they started on the two hundred acres close to the nearby town, Catacamas (Cah-ta-CAH-mas). On Wednesday morning, June 16, the Honduran who lived on that property rushed to El Sembrador.

He met Ted halfway between house and barn. "Campesinos have come and ordered you to stop planting on your property by Catacamas."

Ted ran to the farmhouse porch and threw open the screen door. "Dad," he yelled, "I think you'd better come out here."

Don appeared with Twana and Joanne at his heels. Ted repeated what he had just heard.

"Well," Don exclaimed, "it looks like what we had hoped wouldn't happen is about to, anyway. It's time for action. I'm going to get don Luis and we'll probably go right on to Juticalpa (Hoo-tee-CALL-paw) to see the lawyer and Colonel Padilla (Paw-DEE-yah)."

"That's a good idea," Ted agreed. "He might be helpful in resolving the problem."

Don left with scarcely another word behind him.

Lord, Don prayed as he shifted into second, steering between the deepest ruts. *You know all about this problem. El Sembrador is Yours and I can't believe You'll let it be taken away from us like this. Please take care of the situation.*

The El Sembrador property in question lay east of town at the junction of the two roads. Don slowed the pickup as he approached the partially planted field.

There they are. The campesinos have seen me coming, and it looks like they mean business.

As Don drove closer the Hondurans swarmed onto the road. Each man had a firm grip on his machete, sharp point up, ready for action.

1 9 4 6 – 1 9 5 4

1

Don Hawk jerked dry husks from the large, well-formed ear of corn, a mechanical task that allowed his mind to range far ahead of his hands.

Honduras! David Schneider said God needs lay workers in Honduras. To work with boys, especially. He ought to know; he and Chloe have been missionaries there a long time.

Another ear of corn. Two more...three...

Lord, someone ought to go. I can't get David's message out of my mind.

The cornstalks rustled like paper in the fall breeze. God had given a good crop that summer, 1946.

I've never felt this way about a message before, though I've heard dozens of preachers and been in more missionary meetings than I can count.

Don stepped left. Again his hands moved in the practiced rhythm of an experienced farmer.

Why is my heart pounding?

He rubbed his sweaty palms down the legs of his blue overalls.

You know, Lord, since I heard David's message I've struggled with the idea that...that...that You might be calling me to Honduras. But I have a family. Anyway, I don't have the education necessary for a missionary.

Two more stalks, and another row finished. His livestock would relish this corn.

We have a fine farm here and it's making us a good living. We just got the new Oldsmobile, and...in fact, Lord, there's an awful lot of reasons why we should stay here in Ohio instead of going to Honduras.

Don's mind worked faster than his hands, but it circled around one idea. *Could it be...would...is God calling me to Honduras? To do what I know best...to farm? I can't seem to get away from that idea. But I wonder. Can I really go through with it?*

Two mice, startled out of their quarters, scuttled along the row to safety. Don paid no attention to them.

Honduras...Honduras...Honduras...me, Lord? But I have...

God's talking to me. I know He is.

Don dropped to his knees beside a cornstalk. His thoughts settled. His mind cleared. Before long he said aloud, "Yes, Lord, I don't know what the future will hold, but I want You to have everything. I'll do what You want me to do, come what may."

He opened his eyes and saw his hand holding the ear of corn, raised toward heaven.

Slowly he stood to his feet, taking off his sweat-stained straw hat allowing the breeze to tousle his dark hair. Many years later he would say, "It's a good thing I didn't know what the *come what may* would be," but at that moment, with the unknowns not yet discovered, his spirit expanded with peace. He could hardly wait to tell Twana.

Later we'll explain everything to Teddy, too. And with the new baby coming in a few weeks, that'll mean two little ones to take to Honduras. And there's Charles...we'll need to find another home for him. He's not ready to be on his own yet."

At supper that evening, Don, lean and tan from hard work in summer's sun, looked across the table at his wife. Her thick black hair, always well arranged, and her snappy dark eyes still held appeal. He remembered the first time he noticed Twana Baker, a smiley fourteen-year-old, as she looked his direction from across the sanctuary at the Gregg Street Church of Christ in Christian Union. Later that week he had raised enough nerve to ask, "Will you go with me to the school play Friday night?"

"Yes," she replied.

He smiled as he thought about the fun they had from then on. She even continued to ride his Harley Davidson with him after he had the accident that knocked out his two front teeth.

When the war started, everyone felt the uncertainty as many young men from Washington Court House signed up for military duty. Don, twenty, and Twana, seventeen, knowing neither set of parents would approve their marriage at that time, did what many other couples did in wartime. They eloped. After the ceremony on October 10, 1942, they each went back home to their parents.

They told no one until Twana's graduation day the next spring. "Well," said Mrs. Baker when she heard the news, "if I had known, Don would have paid for all of Twana's graduation expenses."

Juggling those pleasant memories that fall evening in 1946, Don reminded himself, *I always knew Twana was special, but I found out she's even more special than I dared hope for. A city girl to start with, but she's sure adjusted well to farm life.*

He watched her tuck two-year-old Teddy into bed and together they heard his prayers. Don said, "Goodnight, Son," then gave Twana a quick kiss as they left Teddy's room.

Later, after he turned their bedroom light off, Don took a deep breath and asked, "Twana, remember last summer when David and Chloe Schneider were at the missionary meeting at church?"

"Uh-huh. They spoke about the need for lay workers in Honduras. Especially to work with boys."

"Well, I haven't been able to forget David's message. In fact, I've wondered since then if maybe God was calling us to Honduras—to farm. That's what we know best."

Don cleared his throat. "This afternoon out in the corn field, I said a final *yes* to God. I know for certain, Twana, He's calling me to start a farm school for underprivileged boys in Honduras."

Somewhere on a neighboring farm a dog barked. Another answered from farther down the road. Don turned to face Twana and put his arm around her. "What do you think?" he asked.

Her eyes looked into his, and even in the darkness she saw in his handsome face everything the teenage Twana had admired and loved. "I'm your wife," she whispered. "I'll go wherever you think God wants you to go."

Conversation continued long after their usual going-to-sleep time. They hardly knew the location of Honduras. The culture and living conditions remained a mystery. Their talk drifted to what others would think.

As the clock showed the beginning of a new day, Don said, "I still think we did right to invite Charles to live with us. We've given him a good home with stability, and I've seen a big improvement in him."

Don told this young teen from the Gregg Street Church before suggesting he live with them, "You're not really a *bad* boy, Charles, but somehow you manage to get into a lot of trouble. Twana and I want to see you through school and headed in the right direction."

That night as they continued to consider Honduras, Twana suggested, "You surely can help Charles find another suitable home."

Their conversations grew heavy with questions, some with ready-made answers, some with no answers at all. At last Don said, "David and Chloe haven't gone back to Honduras yet. Let's get together with them. I'm sure they can answer our questions."

Like Mary in Bethlehem, Don and Twana kept these thoughts to themselves. They also stayed busy with the usual fall work while preparing for Thanksgiving and the new baby due soon.

Timothy Neal arrived on December 6.

Now the picture of the Hawks in Honduras had grown larger. "And more complicated," Don and Twana told themselves, wondering about life so far away from all things familiar.

2

"**D**on, the best thing would be for you to visit us after we get back to Honduras," said David Schneider. "I could fly you around in our little Gospel Wings plane to help you get the lay of the land."

A few weeks later Don headed south. Not knowing the best route, he rode a bus to Brownsville, Texas, then boarded a plane for Mexico City, changing to another headed for Honduras.

He had scarcely greeted the Schneiders when David said, "We'll need to cover a lot of territory while you're here. We better not waste any time." On horseback, in ox cart and airplane, David gave Don a hurried introduction to World Gospel Mission's ministry in Olancho, a district located east and slightly north of the capital city.

Impressions and ideas interlaced with plans, and back home again in Ohio, Don told Twana, "Now that I've been there, I know for sure we should go. But life in Honduras'll be a lot different for us. It's really primitive out there in Olancho. Like the wild west used to be here in our country."

At last they let others know their plans.

"Honduras? What part of Africa is that in?"

"Honduras is an island, isn't it?"

"Honduras? Why, that's wonderful."

"I admire you for obeying God."

"You mean you're moving that far away? What about your children? I wouldn't want to take my family to a place like that."

"That's quite a sacrifice, a big undertaking."

The Hawk and Baker parents stood firmly behind Don and Twana. "We're praying for you," they promised. Other family members questioned the young couple's boldness. "Don and Twana are crazy for even thinking about taking a family to a foreign country, especially one as undeveloped as where they want to go."

"I know," another relative agreed. "Probably, though, it's just a dream that'll pass."

Setting negative reactions aside, Don and Twana took time in the midst of planting and cultivating to meet with the Churches of Christ in Christian Union (CCCU) Mission Board. "God has called us to Honduras," Don explained. "We plan to farm and start a school for underprivileged boys. A lot of 'em don't have opportunity to go to school. Yet they need some way to learn how to make something of themselves. Girls often go to work for wealthier people and that gives them some opportunity in life, but boys...well, they just don't have much chance. We'll teach 'em to read and write and how to farm better, and along with that we'll teach the gospel message. We'll aim for the farm to support the school."

Board members asked questions and Don answered. Finally, the president said, "Our funds are limited. We can't support something new, especially a project such as you have presented. We will, however, pledge our prayer support, and we'll help you with any technical advice you need. Perhaps you could meet with the board of World Gospel Mission."

Reverend E. A. Keaton, the denominational moderator, suggested, "Don, if you want to start a boys' farm, why don't you consider our CCCU farm just out of Circleville, Ohio? That might be preferable to moving out of the country."

Don shook his head. "Thank you for the offer, but God has called us to Honduras. I've grown up learning that when I feel certain I should do something, there's nothing to do but do it."

Don and Twana drove home, disappointment burdening their spirits. After a few days, Don wrote to Dr. George Warner, World Gospel Mission's president. The reply arrived soon.

Please come to our meeting in Chicago this fall. We would like to hear what you have to say, but I cannot promise you will be considered for missionary appointment. Sincerely, Dr. George Warner.

The day of the board meeting, Don and Twana drove to Chicago in their new Oldsmobile. Their friend, Bob Smith, a missionary to Kenya, rode with them.

"I'm really nervous," said Twana. "What will they think of us?"

"I don't know, but I'm scared too." Don reached over to squeeze Twana's hand. "We have each other and God has called us. He's going to lead us all the way. We know that, so we'll just go in there and tell the board what He wants us to do."

Bob encouraged them. "Your call from God is the most important factor."

They arrived at the meeting site, Chicago Evangelistic Institute. Once inside the lobby Don led the way to a brown leather settee where he and Twana sat down to wait their turn. Tense and uneasy, feeling as if the Big Ones in the next room would devour them, they said nothing. They did not smile.

An older gentleman, relaxed and at ease, rocked back and forth in a high-backed rocker across the room. "Why are you here?" he asked.

"We're going before the World Gospel Mission Board," Don answered.

"Why?"

"God has called us to Honduras, and we're hoping the board will accept us as missionaries."

The rocking chair squeaked softly. "My wife's on the board and I'm waiting for her," said the man. "What do you want to do in Honduras?"

After Don told him, the man asked, "What's Honduras like?"

Don described his recent visit with the Schneiders.

The rocking continued. "Who's going to support you?"

"We plan for the farm to eventually be self-supporting. In the meantime we'll trust the Lord."

The questions kept coming. Don hardly completed one answer before he had to start another.

Meanwhile, behind closed doors sat the group who had authority to decide either for or against the mission's involvement in the Hawk's future.

"Who is this couple, anyway?" asked a businessman.

"Young farmers from Ohio," one woman explained.

"These crazy kids have some notion about teaching better farming methods to young men and boys in Honduras," said another.

"I assume they'll teach them about Christ too," an evangelist noted.

The board secretary sighed and suggested, "Let's call them in."

Entering the meeting room, Don hoped his smile would disguise his nervousness. Twana gripped her purse tightly with both hands. They each took a deep breath and looked around the long conference table at the men and women of great spiritual stature and reputation.

Dr. Warner, sitting at the head of the table, smiled and introduced the board members before he said, "Please tell us, Mr. Hawk, what you want to do."

Don told the story, and when he finished the questions began.

"What exactly is your background?"

After hearing about Hawk's farming experience, their membership in the Gregg Street Church, and their families, another questioner asked, "What is your formal education?"

Once again Don replied clearly, "We have no education beyond high school. We went right into farming with my father and brothers."

"How do you expect to be supported in Honduras?"

Don continued to answer confidently. "We don't have any support, other than what we can do for ourselves. We'll just step out in faith and trust the Lord."

Next, white-haired Dr. Willa Caffrey asked, "And Mrs. Hawk, what about you?"

I'm not going to let her scare me, Twana told herself, straightening her shoulders and looking directly at the formidable woman. "Don is my husband and I am not about to let him go to Honduras alone."

More questions and answers, then at last Dr. Warner said, "Thank you for coming. I'm sure I speak for all the board members when I say our hearts have been deeply touched today."

Heads nodded agreement as Dr. Warner continued. "I sense in you a spirit akin to that of the sainted Livingstone." He paused, looking down at his notes. "No doubt this is a good project you have in mind and a worthy cause, but because of the pressure of other responsibilities, we can't place you under appointment as regular missionaries. We will, however, offer our prayer support and consider you associate missionaries. Also we'll be glad to help you with information about how to ship your goods out of the country and how to get your visas and passports."

"Thank you very much," said Don. "We'll appreciate that because as soon as we can get ready we'll go to Honduras."

He and Twana left the room, not knowing until years later that back in the conference room, Dr. C. I. Armstrong turned to Dr. Caffrey and whispered, "I hope that leaving a big, nice, productive farm in Ohio and going into the jungles of

Honduras isn't something rash they're going to regret. It doesn't look expedient for a man with a family to start off to a strange land."

On their way through the lobby, Don and Twana smiled at the man in the rocking chair. They did not ask his name, leaving with no idea of his eventual importance to their work. Walking to the Oldsmobile, Don said, "I wish the board felt they could give us financial support, but we'll do as we said. We'll step out in faith."

Several weeks later they attended World Gospel Mission's International Convention in Wichita, Kansas. Leaders introduced Don and Twana to the entire congregation, reminding, "This young couple will appreciate your prayers."

That convention began for many a lifetime commitment to pray for Don and Twana Hawk.

3

Plans made and carried out accumulated quickly after the Wichita convention. Passports arrived by mail. Charles Barton moved to another suitable home. Fall harvests ended, followed by the sale to close Hawk's Ohio farming connections.

"Now for some serious packing," said Don. Bob Smith and his wife, Catherine, supported the task with their expert advice. The men built two large wooden crates while Catherine showed Twana and her helpers how to carefully wrap dishes and place them piece by piece in big metal drums.

Twana eyed the new rectangular beige rug. How soft it felt to bare feet. "Let's take it," she suggested. "It'll be so practical when Timmy starts crawling." This one bit of luxury, as she called it, eventually outlived termite-eaten and humidity-damaged furniture. Whether it lay on floors of clay brick, cement tile, or wood, the rug held up under the patter of small Hawk feet, even into the second generation.

Gradually the crates filled with furniture, farm fencing, and kitchen equipment. Small personal items, tools, books, and toys fit snugly in between. Clothes and bedding made wonderful padding. Bags of vegetable seeds fit snugly into leftover spaces.

Next, Don and his brother worked on the new Jeep. They attached a power take-off so a small plow and disk could work off it. "Like a tractor," Don explained. "I might be able to plant the first crop with it." They also attached an extension on the back of the Jeep, making more space for hauling loads.

At last, with all preparations completed and The Unknown looming ahead like a black hole, Don and Twana said goodbye to everything and everyone familiar to them. Don, however, testified clearly, "I still feel right about uprooting our family from here in Ohio and planting it in Honduras."

Early in the cold and blustery morning of December 27, 1947, the four Hawks, plus Teddy's honey-blonde collie named Boo, stuffed themselves into the Jeep with a small trailer hitched behind. Bob and Helen Hawk, Don's brother and wife, along with a family friend, Wayne Forsythe, crowded into the cab of Wayne's farm truck loaded with the crates, metal drums, disk, and plow. The two vehicles turned south, headed for New Orleans.

The New Year had arrived by the time the Jeep and truck pulled into the Jung Hotel's front parking lot. A fashionable hotel in downtown New Orleans, the Jung did not often see such travel-weary folks climbing out of country-type vehicles.

"We're sure a bedraggled looking bunch," Twana muttered.

Don hurried into the hotel to register, knowing his companions longed for a hot meal, warm baths, and comfortable beds. The bellboy quickly escorted Twana and her boys, along with Helen, upstairs to their rooms. The doorman said to the men, "Please park your truck and Jeep around in back out of sight."

A good night's rest revived the travelers.

The next day they drove to the docks to locate the boat and see about getting everything loaded. "You got the papers for your dog?" asked a dock worker.

"Papers?"

"Yeah. He's gotta have his vaccinations before you can take him out of the country."

Don looked at Twana. She looked at their collie, instantly named when seven-month-old Teddy said "Boo" at first sight of the dog. With his tongue hung lazily out the left side of his mouth, Boo pressed tightly against Teddy's right leg and looked eagerly from Don to the unfamiliar man, then licked Teddy's face.

"He hasn't had shots," explained Don. "Nobody told us he needed 'em."

"Guess he can't go, then. There's no time to get 'em now."

Don scratched Boo's ears. Twana gathered Teddy close while Don explained to Teddy and Timmy why Boo could not go with them to their new home. "We're all disappointed, and we'll all miss him." He brightened as he added, "But don't worry. We'll get another dog in Honduras."

Early the next day, Don and Twana made the final break with home as they said goodbye to Bob, Helen, Wayne, and Boo. When the others left, Don put one arm around Twana, who held Timmy, and the other around Teddy. "Well, this is it. Just us four and the Lord, striking out for whatever's ahead."

They boarded the open-decked banana boat, a freighter with space for a few passengers. The excitement of these two young Ohio farmers, ages twenty-five and twenty-two, who had scarcely ridden in a small boat, grew as the big engines rumbled. Slowly, the boat moved away from the dock, starting south toward the Gulf of Mexico.

The first evening, the captain invited them to eat at his table. Don and Twana, used to good, plentiful farm food, stared at the amazing display. Chicken, beef, fish, pork, and potatoes fixed several ways filled platters and bowls. When Twana saw the huge, appealing array of vegetables and salads, she exclaimed, "Oh, my." Then as she surveyed plates of rolls, biscuits, and bread next to sparkling jams and jellies in glass dishes, she shook her head. "I don't know which one I want."

Soon as stuffed as a Thanksgiving turkey, the diners groaned when the captain pointed to three kinds of pie and several cakes disguised under swirls of chocolate, layers of coconut, or fluffy white frostings. "Have what you like," he urged.

They finished dinner and with the boys firmly in hand, Don and Twana strolled the deck before bedtime. "God is so good," they assured each other.

Breakfast the next morning proved more than ample. Afterward Twana frowned, swallowed hard, and muttered, "Oh shoot. We aren't even to the Gulf, and I'm already seasick." At lunch she ate a few bites, wishing later she had stayed in the cabin instead.

"You and the boys go ahead and eat," she told Don as the dinner hour approached. She slid into her bunk that now had too much swing and sway. Fortunately, the metal wastebasket stood within reach.

"I'm sorry," Don comforted when he returned from dinner. "Just lay still. I'll watch the boys." Twana closed her eyes while her husband sat beside her, holding her left hand firmly between his callused hands. He looked at Twana, still beautiful though her dark hair lay in sweaty strands around her gray-green face.

I sure appreciate how she said "I'm married to you. I'll go wherever the Lord calls you." But, have I made a serious mistake? Bringing her away from everything we've ever known and heading off to a strange place where we can't speak the language? And who knows if we'll live in a house or a hut. Maybe we'll only have the sky for a roof over our heads.

Don's thoughts wandered around Anxiety's circle. He steadied the metal wastebasket as Twana coughed, gagged, and retched again and again. More thought-wandering, then the right answer revealed itself to him. *It's never a mistake when one follows God's leading. And that's exactly what I'm doing.*

The same peace he had experienced in the cornfield more than a year before once again cheered his spirit. He dampened a washcloth and wiped Twana's brow. *I'm glad I obeyed God. That's the only way to have real peace.*

The next day after breakfast Don returned to the cabin and flopped onto his bunk. Twana sat up. "You look terrible. Are you seasick too?"

He moaned and reached for the wastebasket.

The rest of the day the wastebasket slid from one bunk to the other. Their kind steward helped, making sure they had what they needed as well as looking after the boys. Next morning, he came to offer help again. He found Twana already up, dressing Timmy. Don sat on the edge of his bunk looking more lively than the previous day. "We're much better," Twana reported.

That day and the next passed uneventfully.

The wind lightly textured the water's surface the last evening aboard the banana boat. As the sun went down, Teddy looked out the porthole. "Oh, Mommy, the sun is melting into the water."

Twana smiled. *That's a perfect description. Thank You, Lord, for what Teddy just said.* To her, his words put a seal on the trip, helping erase the homesickness, sadness, and questioning that had rested heavily upon her as she lay ill.

Finally, they could see the lights of Tela (TAY-la) on the north coast of Honduras. "We'll be here overnight," the captain explained. "Go ashore if you like and look around."

"Let's do," Don suggested. "It's still early. We can send a telegram to the folks in Ohio to let 'em know we're this far, anyway."

He and Twana each carried a little boy as they started down the gangplank. A Honduran met them as they stepped on shore and asked in English-with-an-accent, "Are you going into town?"

"Yes," replied Don.

The man stepped closer and said softly, "It's very dangerous for you to go into town wearing your watches and rings and carrying valuables. You could be robbed. Just leave your things with me, and I'll guard them until you come back."

Don glanced back to the boat. He noticed the first officer looking directly at him, shaking his head vigorously. Suddenly Don understood.

He cleared his throat, looked at the man before him, and said, "No, thanks. We'll get along okay." Only after they had lived in Honduras awhile did Don and Twana fully understand what a good deed the first officer had done for them.

The next afternoon the boat docked at Puerto Cortes. "We'll be here overnight," the captain announced once again. "You're welcome to sleep on board tonight and then find your lodgings tomorrow."

The next morning, the young American family, standing in suspense on the wharf, squinted in the bright sunlight reflecting off the white sand and blue water. Small fishing boats bobbed alongside the stately oceangoing vessels. A few men and boys dangled long sticks with strings to tempt the fish.

"Another milestone in our lives," said Twana with a final look at the banana boat. Later she said, "It was a real nice trip if we hadn't been seasick," but at that moment she declared, "I will never, no never, come down to Honduras again if I have to come by boat."

"We should find a hotel," Don said. "After we get settled I'll make arrangements to get our stuff off the boat." He slung his rifle over one shoulder and held Timmy in the other arm. Twana held Teddy's hand and carried her accordion.

They walked the tracks before they found the path into town. Instantly they felt awash with unfamiliar sights, sounds, and smells.

Brown-skinned, black-haired women, carrying their wares in huge baskets on their heads, clutched toddlers in their arms and pulled along older ones who grabbed their mothers' skirts. Other children, sellers on their own, carried baskets of sweets, bread, the morning's catch of fish, or freshly killed meat.

"Why don't all the kids have clothes on?" whispered wide-eyed Teddy. His parents had no answer as they dodged wandering dogs and donkeys.

Men walked, rode horseback, drove weighty wooden-wheeled ox carts, or pushed smaller, heavily loaded ones.

They all wore large straw hats and carried guns, machetes, or hunting knives.

Teddy, still fascinated with these new sights, observed aloud, "Almost everybody has bare feet."

A chorus of boat whistles, people shouts, bird songs, animal squawks, rustling palm trees, and lapping waves blended together with Spanish words and songs. The clomp, clomp of trotting horses added the staccato.

"I smell meat cooking somewhere," Don said.

Twana sniffed the odorous air. "And beans, too." In time their noses grew accustomed to rich fragrances of roasting coffee and sugar cane at the boil. They also eventually ignored overripe tropical fruits, fish, damp sand, and open sewer-ditch smells.

"Look at those beautiful flowers," Twana said, pointing to yellow, red, purple, and brilliant pink blossoms that mingled over stone walls and beside porches. "I wonder if we'll ever have any like that where we live?" Her appreciation spread to other blooms rambling beneath banana plants, coconut palms, and strange, exotic trees with fruit she did not recognize.

In contrast, the unpainted wooden two-story hotel rose starkly from the gray-brown sandy dirt. No color graced its plainness. The attendant spoke passable English, understanding that Hawks needed a room and assigning one to them. He pointed to Don's rifle. "You will check that here." Don looked at Twana and frowned. Was this the usual routine? Would he get his gun back? With no other option offered, Don shrugged his shoulders and did as the man asked.

They climbed the narrow wooden steps to the second floor and located their room separated from the porch by only a screen door. Inside, a flat cotton mattress topped each bed. A battered dresser hugged the far wall. Twana put her accordion on one bed and sat beside it.

Living in Honduras is going to take some getting used to, she thought. She could not that day have believed how quickly Honduras, the birth-land for their children yet unconceived and for eight of their grandchildren as well, would feel more like home than Ohio. Latins would become their people. Speaking Spanish would become second nature.

Teddy put his hand on Twana's knee. "Mommy, I want a drink."

She headed for the tall bottle and three glasses on the dresser. "Here's some water," Twana said. She picked up a glass in one hand and the bottle with the other, tipping it to pour. At the same time someone pounded on their screen door.

"Don't drink that water," a voice yelled.

Twana almost dropped the bottle. "Don, what's going on?"

Her husband stepped to the door. "Well, what do you know. Dave Schneider! What in the world are you doing here? Come on in."

"I had it figured out about when you'd get in, so I thought I'd fly up and give you a hand. Say, Twana, it's a good thing you didn't drink that water. It hasn't been boiled. No telling what parasites might be in it that would've caused you some miserable stomach upsets. Here, let's go downstairs and I'll buy some soda pop for you. That's a lot safer to drink."

Dave led the way back down the wooden steps. "There's a commercial flight leaving for Tegucigalpa this afternoon. If we hurry we can make it. I'll go on the flight with you and get you settled in the mission guest house and introduce you to the missionaries. They're having their annual conference right now."

"But what about our things on the ship?" Don asked.

"You and I'll drive back later and get everything."

"You know what you're doing, so whatever you say is fine with us. Right, Twana?"

She nodded. "I should say. I've never seen anyone look as good as you did a while ago. We didn't know how we were going to manage without help."

Hawks checked out of their unused room, collected Don's rifle, and hurried off to the airstrip located along the beach.

They purchased tickets on SAHSA, an airline they soon came to know well.

After a smooth takeoff at the water's edge the army surplus DC-3 rose above the waves and circled over the mountains toward the capital city. Twana glanced at Don and Teddy while Timmy rested quietly on her lap. *Well, at least we've come safely this far. But my, so much to think about already. I wonder what's next.*

4

Sixteen World Gospel Mission (WGM) missionaries smiled at the four Hawks when David Schneider introduced them.

"Welcome to our annual field conference," said the man at the far end of the room. "I'm Ellery Echlin, Honduras field superintendent. We missionaries meet together two times a year."

After a round of introductions, Mr. Echlin said, "Mr. and Mrs. Hawk, we look forward to getting acquainted with you. Before we conclude our meetings we'll want to hear from you, but we'll give you a chance to catch your breath first."

The missionaries continued their discussions, motions, and votes. Before adjournment, Mr. Echlin asked, "Would someone make a motion that we invite the Hawks to sit in on the remaining business sessions of this conference?"

When the motion carried, Don smiled at Twana and she returned his smile. This early acceptance into missionary fellowship soon turned these unfamiliar names and faces into trusted coworkers and lifetime friends.

Mr. Echlin called on Don and Twana in a later business session. "We're glad you're here, and we're anxious to know what you plan to do in Honduras."

Don began their story. "For some time now...."

A few missionary amens and one louder "Praise the Lord" punctuated his explanation and his summary. "So at last we're here with two goals. The main one is to bring Christ to the boys. The other is to improve their quality of life, and the best way to do that is to teach them how to work and how to do for themselves."

He turned to Twana. "Do you have anything to add?"

She remained seated as her dark eyes scanned the group. "Don and I want to cooperate with you folks in every way."

An experienced missionary wiped her eyes. "Mr. and Mrs. Hawk, you've made a big impression on us. It's obvious you've come to do God's will even though you don't know exactly what you're getting into."

In the days that followed, the Hawks completed business. They also made plans for David and Don to fly back to Puerto Cortes, pick up the Jeep and trailer, and drive to Juticalpa, where Schneiders lived.

"But I'll charter a SAHSA plane to take the rest of your cargo out," said David.

"That's a good idea," Don replied. "We've got seven tons of crates and equipment. Thanks for renting a house for us, though I want to start looking for the right farm as soon as I can."

"Twana, you and Teddy and Timmy can fly to Juticalpa on another SAHSA flight with Chloe and our girls." David's organization made it sound simple.

The next day the DC-3 landed and taxied on a bumpy cow-pasture called the Juticalpa Airport. Several Honduran Christians stood alongside to greet the arrivals. They oohed and ahed over the two little boys. "Gringitos," several said as they timidly touched pale arms. At that moment, the Hawk boys did not know what to think about the unexpected attention. *They're probably too scared to cry,* Twana thought. In the weeks to come, however, her sons grew to enjoy the special notice Hondurans gave them.

Twana, Chloe, and their greeters watched as men loaded the missionaries' baggage onto an ox cart. As soon as the driver urged the oxen toward the road the people, too, started walking the mile back to town. The Schneider girls, Mary

Martha and Karolyn, skipped ahead with their friends. Two young men hoisted Teddy and Timmy onto their shoulders.

The sun, nearly at the height of its daytime travels, made Twana wipe her face again and again. *I thought the temperature in Tegucigalpa was really nice, but the heat here in Olancho is a different story.*

"I'm glad you and the boys will stay with us until the men get back with your things," said Chloe. "That's our house there." She pointed to a whitewashed adobe brick house roofed with clay tile much the same as all the others within sight.

From the cobblestone street they entered the big main door of the Schneider home. The young men lowered Teddy and Timmy onto the brown clay brick floor to stand beside their mother while Chloe and her daughters greeted several Honduran women who shyly watched from the kitchen.

"They're from the church," she explained. "They've prepared dinner for us. Let me introduce you to them."

"Buenas tardes, señora," each woman respectfully said to Twana, who already recognized this midday greeting. She could easily understand their hand gestures as Chloe said, "They want us to sit right down at the table. Dinner is ready."

Twana and the boys ate well at their first real Honduran meal. "This is good," said Teddy, scooping up the last bite of chicken and rice.

"Here, Twana," Chloe encouraged, "have more platanos."

Twana helped herself. "I've never had cooked bananas before."

"They're different than you have in the States, all right. I'll show you how to fix them."

They all reached for more freshly made corn tortillas, slices of fried yucca, and cabbage salad. "Does the yucca remind you of American fried potatoes?" Chloe wanted to know.

Twana nodded. "Everything tastes wonderful."

"The women are smiling. They can tell you're enjoying the meal, and they're delighted. It's the kind of dinner they prepare for someone special."

With that meal, Honduran food became a Hawk favorite.

In a few days, the SAHSA flight with Hawks' belongings arrived at the cow-pasture airport. Don and David drove in later that week.

Twana listened eagerly as Don picked up the boys and at the same time explained, "We met a man who works in the Department of Hacienda. He made it possible to get all our stuff into the country duty-free! We didn't have to pay a thing. Well, that is except the sixty dollars they charged for your accordion. Isn't that something?" He looked as pleased as a boy showing his nickel purchase at the fair.

Twana thought about the money they had brought along, remembering it needed to last a long time. *Thank You, Lord, for this miracle.*

"The officials really welcomed Don when they found out you folks are coming as agriculturists," David said. "The Hondurans are interested in learning more about farming."

Right away Don and Twana moved their household goods into the rented house on the same street as Schneiders', four blocks away at the opposite side of the town plaza. They noticed their Honduran neighbors whispering whenever the Norte Americanos appeared. "They act like they're talking about us," Twana mentioned to Chloe. "What are they saying?"

"They think you're brave to rent this house. It's been vacant a long time. No one wanted to live here."

"Why?"

"Because people are superstitious," Chloe replied. "A doctor once lived here, and one night his enemies came to the door and murdered him right here in the house."

"You mean we have a haunted house?" Twana laughed.

"That's what the people think."

"Well, we're not concerned. This house meets our needs just fine until we locate a farm."

Overlooking the darksome reputation, the two Ohio farmers began daily life in Honduras. They unpacked and laid down the lovely beige rug. Twana quickly learned that grocery shopping meant going one place to buy vegetables, another for meat, then someplace else for bananas. Once home with the food, she carefully soaked and washed the fresh vegetables in disinfectant. Don helped cut big hunks of meat into small roasts or grind them into hamburger.

They bought water three boys and their donkey hauled from the nearby river. Twana then boiled it at least twenty minutes, making it safe for family use.

Chloe helped make arrangements for household help. "We missionaries all hire local girls or women to help us," she explained. "Otherwise we would have no time to do our missionary work."

Every morning, Hilda, a local school girl, collected Twana's shopping list, took it to Chloe for translation, and then hurried from shop to shop to buy the items. A woman picked up from the Hawk house the daily dirty diaper accumulation. At day's end she returned it, dry, folded, and sun-bleached to a whiteness no American soap dared promise.

Don and Twana hired a young woman named Maria, inviting her to live in one of their small rooms. She watched, listened, and soon practiced her new American cooking and cleaning skills learned from Twana. Maria also taught Twana the basics of Honduran cooking. As they cooked and cleaned together, they shared their languages. Trials and errors preceded proficiency.

"Buenos dias, muchachas," Twana greeted the three water boys when they halted their donkey at her door one morning.

The boys raised their eyebrows and rolled their eyes at one another. The tallest one giggled and hitched up his pants as he said, "Muchachas? No. MuchachOS."

Twana looked puzzled. Suddenly she laughed, embarrassed. "Oh! Si. Muchachos. Of course you're not girls."

Hawks learned to do as their neighbors did every evening. The adults stood or sat outside on the sidewalk and visited with each other while their children played in the street. Leaning against her door, not knowing enough Spanish to say much, Twana had time to consider these Hondurans: dark skinned, but with a wide range of color—suntanned white, rich caramel, coffee with a dab of cream, or chocolate pudding. No two heads of hair looked the same either: dusky brown or inky black, straight, wavy, curly, kinky. One listless boy's hair reminded her of dull copper. "A sign of malnourishment," Chloe said. Twana noticed round faces, long faces, and some with high cheekbones. *I wish I could tell each one of them about God's love.*

These leisurely evenings outside helped Don and Twana gradually become better acquainted with neighboring families. While Twana learned kitchen conversation, Don found out names of several farmers. From them he absorbed all he could about seasons, weather, farming methods, and local crops.

"I think I know enough now to start buying and selling grains," he said after a few weeks. "I'll buy rice and beans and corn out here in Olancho, load up our trailer, and drive into the capital to sell them. That'll give us money toward our support and some for supplies too."

"That's a good idea," Twana agreed. "The money we brought with us won't buy everything we need and property too."

The overland trips into Tegucigalpa required detailed planning, though the family seldom made the trip with Don. Usually Twana sent her list with him, soon becoming an expert at long-distance shopping.

When the family did go, Twana packed generous amounts of sandwiches, bananas, boiled water, powdered milk, and cookies. She made sure they took blankets and jackets, "in case we get caught in the mountains at night," rubber boots, and anything else the boys might need.

The trip from Juticalpa to Tegucigalpa could take twelve to fourteen hours or even two or three days, depending on weather, conditions of fordable rivers, frequency of flat tires, and other unexpected variables. Only a narrow trail wound its way through the jungle from Juticalpa to Campamento. From there into the capital, a rutty dirt road climbed up the east side of one steep forested mountain range, wound down the west side, then up and down again three more times through short valleys that separated the four mountain ranges. Many rivers caused additional handicaps along the tortuous route.

Participating in Sunday services at the Schneider residence brought Don and Twana in close contact with Hondurans. Twana sometimes played the little portable pump organ. Even with their limited Spanish they enjoyed activities with the young people's group led by fourteen-year-old Manuel Figueroa.

After they returned one evening from taking the youth to an open air meeting, Twana said as she put away her accordion, "That Manuel is certainly an intelligent young man. A staunch Christian too."

"He spends a lot of time at the Schneider home," said Don. "They say he's read most of the books they have at their house. He's taught himself how to type on their typewriter too."

"No doubt he'll make something of himself some day."

With no property to call their own as yet, Don and Twana told each other, "Faith and patience are the lessons we need to learn right now."

Before long someone told them about a little plot for sale along the Juticalpa River. They bought it and arranged for a Christian family to move into the small house. Don set up his tiny farm operation, even buying several hogs.

He and Twana kept their eyes and ears open for a site suitable for the farm school they longed to open. At last they found a place at the base of the mountains northeast of Juticalpa, near the Telica River. "It's ideal," they agreed.

"But you're asking too much money for it," Don told the owner. "If you'll come down ten dollars, we'll take it."

The man took his time before replying. "I'll come down five dollars."

"I won't go up the five dollars to meet your price. That's too much. I'll go home over the weekend and come back next week to talk about it again."

The next day Don received a direction-changing message from Arthur Schnasse, World Gospel Mission missionary located in Catacamas, a few miles east of Juticalpa.

5

Meet me at the airport next Wednesday. I'll be on my way to Tegucigalpa, and I want to tell you about a farm that's for sale near here. I think you folks might be interested.

"Maybe this is our answer, Twana."

As suggested, the two men met at the airport. Arthur explained, "This place I have in mind is eight hundred acres located about six miles southeast of Catacamas. It's almost all jungle, but it's level land that would be farmable after you clear it. One advantage is that the Talgua River flows for nearly three miles through the property. If you and Twana are interested, I'll set a time with don Pedro Morales—he's the owner—and take you out there to look it over."

"We'd like to see it. Just let us know when."

At nine o'clock one morning the next week, the four Hawks and a young friend, José Peck, set off in the Jeep for the two-hour, thirty-mile trip east to Catacamas. Sunshine and blue sky decorated with feathery cloud fragments made a perfect day to travel deeper into the Olancho jungle territory. The trail, barely wide enough for the Jeep, wound around farms and through a swamp. Tropical birds called and whistled while monkeys played overhead in connecting branches. Small wild animals dodged through the underbrush.

Heavily forested mountains to the north stood in three dimension like rows of cardboard cutouts, one behind another—tall, taller, tallest. Steep spiney ridges rose vertically like sharp backbones.

"Since this is the dry season I don't think we're in danger of getting stuck today," Don assured the others. "Anyway, we've got the 4-wheel drive and the winch, too, just in case."

A few miles later, confidence turned into concern.

At three o'clock that afternoon, travel schedule askew, the mud-coated Hawk Jeep pulled into Catacamas, sheltered at the foot of the mountains. Don explained, "We got stuck in an innocent-looking mudhole. The 4-wheel drive was useless since we were in so deep, and there weren't any trees close enough for us to use the winch. Fortunately, José knew a farmer who lives not far from there. He brought his oxen over and they pulled us out."

"The modern and the primitive hitched together did the job," said Twana. Had they known, they could scarcely have believed that fifty years later travelers covered that same route, by then paved, in thirty minutes.

Anticipation swelled inside Don and Twana as the next day's light dawned. Many questions, both spoken and unspoken, flew through their minds.

"Let's go," suggested Arthur. "I told don Pedro we would come before noon." The Schnasses crowded into the Jeep with the Hawk family, Arthur sitting in front to direct the way. At the eastern end of Catacamas, he pointed to the tiny dirt airstrip on the left. "SAHSA DC-3s land there," he said. "That's been handy for us. Now, Don, take this trail that goes off to the right."

The ox cart trail, sometimes wide, sometimes narrow, lengthened out like a poorly drawn line between the dense growth of hard, thorny carbon bushes. "Carbon's great for fence posts and firewood," Arthur noted. "But watch out. It'll grab you, and those thorns really scratch."

He turned toward Don. "I often say this Olancho district is a land flowing with milk and honey. These virgin jungles produce animal products and timber of many kinds. Rubber,

coffee, vanilla, cocoa, and a lot of medicinal plants grow pro-
fusely also. But it's a desert, spiritually speaking. Sin in all its
forms is the curse of both young and old. Irene and I are glad
you've answered the Lord of the harvest and have come out
to help give the Water of Life to this desert."

Deep ruts and mudholes tossed the Jeep like a canoe on
rolling waves. "Your vehicle is ideal out here," Arthur
observed. More bounces and jolts, then he advised, "Turn left
just past this next bunch of carbon. The house is about a mile
on east."

The Jeep bumped along through more carbon that crowded the trail until at last an island of civilization appeared. A
small gray adobe brick house stood at the edge of a partially
cleared area. Ducks, chickens, and turkeys scattered noisily.
Horses hitched to crude posts on the wide porch flicked their
ears and tossed their heads. A smiling Honduran man stepped
out from inside. "Buenos dias," he said.

Arthur quickly responded, "Buenos dias, don Pedro."

Once out of the Jeep, Teddy and Timmy clung tightly to
their mother's dress while the Schnasses and Moraleses con-
versed genially. Don and Twana entered in with smiles.

The fowls settled down and continued their foraging. Pigs,
penned on the east side of the house, grunted as several dogs,
tails waving, nosed around the newcomers. Before long the
three men mounted the horses and set off for their tour.

"We women can stay here and take advantage of these
hammocks," Irene Schnasse suggested.

The little boys bravely ventured a few steps each direction
as Twana rested, allowing her eyes to record the picture before
her. A wide, open corridor or porch, ten feet wide, circled the
small two-room house as if holding it together in a secure
package. Posts anchored into the porch floor helped support
the red tile roof that extended over the corridor. They also
anchored the hammocks and served as hitching posts. A large
cedar box of grain stood against one wall. Stalks of ripening
bananas hung from the rafters above two cows that lay

methodically chewing their cuds on the north porch. From somewhere inside the house, a hen announced her daily egg.

Trees with red flowers high atop their spreading branches reminded Twana of giant bouquets. Yellow, white, and pink flowers decorated other trees too. The jungle pressed in from all sides as if intent on reclaiming its own.

It's really beautiful out here, she thought. *And so peaceful looking.*

When the horseback riders returned, Twana knew by Don's smile that what he had seen pleased him. "This is the place," he confirmed. "We rode across the river and all around the acreage. There's quite a bit of good timber, tropical cedar and mahogany especially, that would certainly be useful when we get ready to build. The land is pretty level, like Arthur said, and even though it'll be hard work to get it ready, it can be done."

Don stretched his arms in a wide gesture. "Nothing's been cleared yet except this small tract behind the house—about an acre, I'm guessing. Arthur translated for us, and don Pedro and I made an agreement."

Sweat made Don's face shine like a polished apple. Twana shaded her eyes from the sunlight's glare as she listened to him.

"We can rent the place for a year with the option to buy it for fifty-six hundred dollars at the end of the year. That's seven dollars an acre. If we do decide to buy, the rent we've paid will apply to the purchase price. We can go ahead and begin to plant corn here among the stumps when the rains start the last of May or first of June. That's what don Pedro planned to do."

Twana mentally calculated, *This is already April, so that means the rains start in only a few weeks. We'll have to move out here almost immediately.*

"Then, too," Don continued, "don Pedro will sell us all his livestock—fifty-two head of cattle and eighty hogs along with chickens, ducks, turkeys, and horses. He'll even throw in the dogs for free. The hired men will stay on too. They're used to milking, and they'll be good help when we start to clear the land."

Don stopped and waited as eagerly as the night he asked her to marry him. "What do you think, Twana?"

She looked into the dark eyes of this courageous man who stood before her at the edge of an enormous challenge. Twana knew Don understood that living out here, 75 miles from the nearest road and 155 miles from the capital city, meant rigorous travel. He realized what it would take to clear 799 acres of jungle, and of course he had seen this tiny, old, unpromising house, crumbling roof tiles and all.

Still, she understood that comfort and convenience meant little compared to complete obedience to God. Love filled her eyes and her smile. "I think you did the right thing, Don."

That day they made a commitment as enduring as their marriage vows. This house in varying forms would shelter them for thirty years, and after that the second and third generations would continue life within its walls and surroundings.

6

ate Saturday afternoon, May 8, Don groaned. "Whew! This is the last load. I've gone back and forth from here to Juticalpa so many times this week I think I could do it with my eyes closed."

He took off his cap, pulled out a blue bandanna, and wiped the dripping perspiration. "They say this is the hottest time of the year, and right now, Twana, I believe it. As soon as I transport the Morales family and their stuff into Catacamas, I'll be back to help get things set up here."

Lantern light made a bright dent in the midnight-dark before Twana saw Don again. "Let's finish up for tonight as quick as we can," she urged.

"We'll need the cookstove about first thing, so let's put it here on the southwest corner of the porch. The stovepipe'll work okay as the chimney."

A large box could function as a table and several chairs fit near the stove. Next, Don and Twana set up the beds in the 8' by 14' east room. This crowded bedroom had one big double door as well as a window that opened eastward. They placed their remaining furniture and Twana's pretty rug in the 8' by 14' room on the west side. Throughout the house, walls 16 inches thick supported heavy rafters, open with no ceilings.

Twana observed aloud, "I guess we're in business."

Her eyes moved from one side of their new quarters to the other. *We've left behind a life of utmost wealth,* she thought. Even their Juticalpa house seemed luxurious in comparison to this one with no electricity, no running water, no inside bathroom, no kitchen cupboards, no pretty curtains, and no privacy. Still, she felt no regrets.

Early the next morning, Maria baked fresh bread for breakfast, picked up eggs as soon as the hens laid them, and broke them into the frying pan. She poured milk straight from the bucket into plastic glasses, and the new farm residents sat down around the table to ask the blessing.

Birds chattered overhead and monkeys bent tree branches low with their gymnastics while Don thanked God for their food, "the freshest anyone could ask for."

Immediately after the "Amen," Teddy yelled, "Mommy, the duck wants my egg."

Maria stomped and flapped her arms at the big white duck until he fled with an indignant quack. A long-legged rooster strutted up to investigate, liked what he saw, and flew onto the table.

"Timmy, eat your food before the chickens get it," his mother advised.

"Oh, oh," said Don. "There's a pig coming this way."

Everyone giggled. Finally Don sputtered, "At least the cows have gone out to pasture so *they* aren't up here vying for our food."

More laughs and then Twana said, "Of course the animals furnished most of the food for our breakfast, so why not help us eat it too. I've never had a Mother's Day breakfast like this before. I don't think I'll ever forget it."

That humorous beginning quickly faded into everyday life as the Hawks had never experienced in Ohio.

The farm animals roamed the jungle during daytime. At night they assembled in the narrow clearing around the house. When it rained all the cattle clomped onto the ten-foot-wide clay-tile porch and huddled together under the overhanging roof.

One morning Twana complained, "What a mess! Don, we've got to get a fence around this house as soon as possible."

The following week, Ellery Echlin rode his motorcycle from Tegucigalpa to Olancho. "We sure appreciate you making that long trip way out here," Don told him. "Even though we're only associates with World Gospel Mission, we feel accepted by you missionaries here in Honduras. That means a lot to us."

Don and Ellery tore the packing crates apart and built walls to enclose the kitchen end of the porch. That job finished, they created a small room for Maria at the opposite side of the open porch, the southeast end. The space between her room and the Hawks' kitchen-eating area turned into the dining room for the hired men.

Ellery also helped Don cut bamboo, split it, and build a fence around the house. "Good," pronounced Twana when she strolled along the fence. "I'm glad those cows can't spend any more nights on the porch."

At bedtime either Don or Twana made sure someone had collected that day's eggs. Finally Twana declared, "Maria says Hondurans let hens lay their eggs in the house so animals won't get the eggs, but these hens will just have to find somewhere else to lay their eggs." Later she discovered the old hens also considered the bedroom a suitable nesting place at hatching time.

Listening to the exposed rafters creak on rainy nights, Don said, "I wonder how long they'll stay up? Hear that stuff falling up there? The termites are chewing the wood. That reminds me of the sign at the Tegucigalpa mission house. Remember? It said, 'Be careful and don't bother the termites because they're holding hands and that's what's holding this building up.'"

With Maria's help, Twana kept the hired men and the family fed well. The men often shot a deer for fresh meat, and Twana discovered the good flavor of guatusa meat. "I had no idea a member of the rodent family could be good to eat," she said.

She grew accustomed to the large variety of bananas. Chatas, platanos, manzana, apple-banana, and the smaller ones familiar to housewives in the United States, all tasted deliciously sweet cooked or uncooked.

Twana mastered the tortilla-making process. She and Maria cooked the large, white, field corn kernels in lime water, then washed and drained them. "Look at that," Twana said. "The hulls fell right off the kernels."

"Si, señora, the lime water loosened them." After that, the women ground the corn, adding a little water to make a stiff dough, which they kneaded before pinching off small portions to roll into round balls. Their hands slapped each ball flat, and with fingers of one hand and the palm of the other hand formed thin rounds. A final patting made each round about five inches across. Cooked on the stovetop, fresh for each meal, the tortillas accompanied rice and beans.

An old nag, loaded with two square water-tight mahogany kegs, plodded up and down the path each day, hauling river water to store in the 55-gallon metal drums beside the house. Bath time meant a short walk to the river. Dense growth beyond the fence offered adequate privacy for other necessities.

"The jungle's so thick out there that if you go out a hundred yards from the house and turn around twice you would be completely lost," Don cautioned.

While Twana blended American and Honduran housekeeping, Don calculated the best way to clear the jungle. The plow or disk hooked onto the Jeep proved useless.

"There's just not enough space to maneuver between the big trees," Don explained. "It's a lot different than I thought."

Don and his hired men, including don Pedro's son, Victor Morales, hacked at trees, branches, and underbrush with machetes and axes and afterward attacked roots with the new picks and shovels. Some stumps had such deep tap-roots the workers could not remove them.

"We'll get them next year," Don said. "It's almost time now to start planting."

One morning Don yelled from outside the fence, "Twana, come take my picture."

She hurried out, camera in hand. Don stood beside a stump twice his height and many feet around at the base. "I have a feeling," he remarked, "it's going to take more than one season to burn this thing down to ashes." As it turned out, that stump needed two dry seasons before it burned enough for the men to grub out its remains.

By mid-June they had cleared enough ground to plant corn. Don furnished the men with long, pointed sticks, gourds, and tin cans. Some jabbed the sticks into the ground to make holes. Others filled their gourds or cans with corn, dropped a few kernels into the holes, then pushed the dirt over them with their feet.

"Well, Twana, we've got almost two acres planted," Don announced later. "Remember the new four-row corn planter we bought last year? That thing planted nearly five hundred acres for us." Don's eyebrows raised as he chuckled. "But then I guess we've done pretty well here with our eight-footed four-row corn planter. You know, that's four men planting alongside each other."

Twana laughed, happy for the humor Don often mixed with his labor.

They planted their American garden seeds in tiny spaces between stumps and stacked tree limbs. "It'll be a regular scavenger hunt when all these vegetables are ready for picking," Don prophesied.

"But they'll make a good addition to our diet."

As fresh, green shoots appeared along the uneven ground, Don and his helpers cut weeds with machetes, a tedious job that made the farm couple admit to one another, "We've taken on an awful big task."

Don continued to buy and sell grains, produce, and coffee. Several times in the next weeks he loaded the trailer and headed to Tegucigalpa to sell his goods or exchange them for gasoline, staples, fencing, and other supplies.

Twana awoke one day, her teeth chattering like a jack-hammer. "Oh, my," she groaned. "I must have a fever. I feel terrible. Every inch of me aches." She wrapped the blanket tightly around her. "I can't get warm." The bed shook, even after Don tucked several more blankets around her.

The fever, chills, and aches continued. Three days passed and Twana's fever rose higher. "It's 104 degrees," said Don. "I'm going to send word to Schnasses to come. Maybe they'll know what's wrong."

Arthur and Irene heeded the message. Taking one look at Twana, buried beneath the blankets, they said, "Since there's no doctor at Catacamas, you should go to the hospital in Tegucigalpa."

Don glanced at the calendar. "This is Friday. The SAHSA plane'll come in from the coast today, so we'd better try to get to Catacamas in time for that flight. The Jeep's not working now, but I'll have our hired man, Alfonso, bring the oxen in from the field and harness them to the cart. Arthur, if you'll help me, we'll put the boys' beds in to make the ride more comfortable for them and Twana."

"You'll need to stretch a tarp over the top to protect 'em from the sun."

They fixed the makeshift ambulance, then Don saddled his big white horse. "I'll ride on ahead, Alfonso, and see if the pilot'll wait for you if he gets ready to go before you get there."

Don galloped out of sight as the ox cart pulled onto the trail. Two chocolate-boys lay on one bed, enjoying their nearly-melted candy bars, gifts from American grandparents. Twana lay on the other bed, more miserable than ever.

Alfonso prodded the oxen to step fast, then faster. One large mudhole after another bounced the cart and tipped it from side to side. Twana's groans increased with each bounce. "Ohhhhh. This is awful. Oh, my. Ohhhhh!"

Fear bleaching his dark skin, Alfonso peered beneath the sheltering tarp. "Señora, I'm so sorry. I'm so sorry. Please don't die."

As quickly as the cart jerked to a stop at the airstrip, Don carefully lifted Twana aboard the plane while Arthur and Irene took charge of the boys, the cart, and the horse. Immediately the pilot shut the door and revved the motor for take-off. Seconds later the ground dropped away as the plane nosed into the sky.

At Juticalpa, the first stop, the North American pilot told Don, "We'll have to take you folks off while we make some shuttle trips to Gualaco and Manto, just over that first ridge of mountains. It won't take us long, then we'll come back and pick you up."

Two workers from a road crew saw Don carry Twana off the plane. One offered, "You can lay her on a cot in our tent, if you want to."

Don settled Twana, still fiery with fever, on a cot inside the tent. The men offered cups of hot chocolate. Before long, Twana broke into a drenching sweat. "I think my fever's broken," she whispered.

"The hot tent, the hot chocolate, and the hot sun all worked for your good, I guess."

"I don't know, but I feel better already."

In Tegucigalpa, Don took Twana directly to the hospital. The doctor reported after doing a blood test, "You've got malaria, Señora Hawk."

Quinine shots quickly brought recovery.

Don and Twana both suffered bouts of chronic malaria for several years. That first time, however, alerted them to symptoms and remedies. They needed no more hospital trips when fever, chills, and aching overtook them.

September days meant harvest.

"Look at these beautiful ears of corn," said Don.

"They're as nice as any I've ever seen," Twana replied. "And look at these onions. I'm sure they each weigh a pound." She also showed him the pile of cabbages, large and firm. Tomatoes, green peppers, beets, carrots, collard greens, rutabagas, kohlrabi, and celery filled one corner of the cramped kitchen.

They looked at each other and nodded. Virgin soil, potash, and good rain had given a fine reward for hard work.

7

"Cristo me ama, Cristo me ama. Cristo me ama, La Biblia dice asi." The timeless truth, "Jesus loves me, the Bible tells me so," rang tunefully from the Hawk porch on Sunday evenings.

Reading the words Twana wrote with chalk on the gray adobe walls, the farm neighbors followed Don's strong voice and Twana's accordion, repeating the same hymns and choruses week after week. Sometimes David and Chloe or the Schnasses drove out to preach a short message, but otherwise the services remained simple with only singing.

"I'll be glad when our Spanish improves enough so we can preach," said Don before one service.

"At least maybe our presence here will be a good witness for the Lord. Don, did you notice how well Teddy and Timmy are singing the songs in Spanish now?"

"They're really learning the language fast. But, the other day I heard Teddy say something I wasn't sure about, so last Sunday I asked Arthur what it meant." Don shook his head and frowned. "When he told me what Teddy had said, I was embarrassed. I know he heard it from the hired men, but I told him not to ever say that again."

"Oh dear. I guess that's a reminder we all had better watch our words."

An afternoon breeze gently swung the 1949 calendar back and forth on its nail hammered into the packing crate kitchen wall. *A whole year in Honduras,* Twana mused. *We've learned a lot, but we've got a long way to go.*

Their dream of a school for underprivileged boys remained bright as the midday sun, though carbon and trees of all sizes still claimed most of the property. Primitive every-day living had narrowed into a defined routine: clearing, plant-ing, buying, selling, cooking, and most of all, learning. Travel, no matter where, consumed hours or days.

"Actually," Don remarked once, "it's the same distance from our house to Catacamas as it was from our farm to Washington Court House. Six miles."

"But here," said Twana, "it takes us an hour of horseback riding to get into town"

They understood more fully the common saying, "The only way to get anywhere in Honduras is either on two feet, four feet, or by plane."

The money they had brought with them dwindled alarm-ingly. "We're down to pretty thin scratching," Don said, look-ing at his account book.

"I'm so thankful our Sunday school class back at Gregg Street Church regularly sends money," said Twana. "Of course other churches do too. It sure helps."

Occasionally they received a check from A.L. Luce. *Use the money however you need it,* the accompanying notes said. *Write to us. If you don't, how can I know what you need?*

"Who is A.L. Luce, anyway?" Don and Twana asked them-selves.

When they questioned Ellery Echlin, he explained, "A.L. Luce owns the Blue Bird Body Company in Fort Valley, Georgia. He's a good friend of our mission. I encourage you to write to him."

Contentment filled their days, even when challenges appeared beyond them. "It's times like these that God's closer than a brother," said Don. "I suppose if we had lots of things we *don't* have, maybe we wouldn't trust the Lord as much as we do now when we really *have* to trust Him for our needs."

"Maybe so. Anyway, He's surely been good to us."

The landscape and its creatures with both beauty and novelty continually surprised and delighted Twana. Great clumps of purple orchids nestled in the branches of its host, the guanacaste (gwanaCOSTaye) tree at the southeast corner of the house. Tiny white orchids on thin stems hung gracefully like ribbons from other branches. More colorful blooms Twana could not identify peeked out from behind leaves.

In April and May, the guanacaste trees with bark like elephant hide streaked with dark, dropped huge, round brown seed pods that curled as if a playful hand had given them a half twist. Inside, hard black seeds the size of big dry beans lay imbedded in a sticky white layer. Don learned from his hired men that these pods made good, nutritious food for the cows.

Big and little toads sang their alto, tenor, and bass choruses loudly, especially during rainy times that also brought the flies. Monkeys romped in trees along the river and by the house, as well. Raccoons, big and little rodents, small mountain lions, little tigers called tigres, and deer lived in the dense jungle. The lions and tigres tried stealing the Hawk calves, but shots by alert workers kept them back. Snakes of various lengths might show up anytime, anywhere, inside or out. Ticks of many kinds burrowed beneath human skin. Mosquitoes, cockroaches, bees, wasps, and hornets showed no discrimination about who, when, and where to attack.

Oblong hornet nests like gray-white paper and pointed at the bottom end swayed high in several trees near the house. The big black blobs on trees or fence posts, Twana learned, housed termites.

Mountains lay in every direction, more easily seen to the north and west. Morning mist or fog sometimes played hide and seek with them. At other times, green, brown, or blue shadows created different pictures. Against a golden sunset sky, the top line of the western mountains appeared as a dark line on a graph.

"Such beauty," Twana said.

The Honduran people also appeared beautiful to Don and Twana. *They've become our friends and family here,* Twana wrote to their families in Ohio. The Hawks' circle of acquaintances gradually enlarged on Sunday afternoons. With Twana's accordion and Irene's flannelgraph board, the Hawks and Schnasses headed for El Real, Jutiquile, Punare, Arimis, or other villages for open-air meetings. Two or three believers often went along to help.

Some village squares had a large tree suitable for shading a group. Friendly families sometimes offered a commodious porch. As accordion music drifted like dust through the village, a crowd quickly gathered. Little boys, wearing suspendered pants and broad-brimmed straw hats pushed their way close to the music source. Their big and little sisters, often lugging another younger child, found unclaimed space for themselves. Fathers and mothers stood around the edge, some eager to hear, some skeptical.

Not everyone welcomed these meetings. The Hawks and the Schnasses, however, carried on in the midst of priestly opposition or drunken interference. "I'm glad God's working and people are getting saved at these meetings," Don said. Later, the missionaries thanked the Lord for the established congregations that developed in these villages.

Don and Twana gradually learned to know their Honduran neighbors. When he had time, Don liked to walk a short distance south to the tiny village, El Carbon. He quickly memorized family names, stopping to chat. Mamas always offered cups of hot, strong coffee they soon discovered he liked.

There he met José Hernandez. "You say you're ten years old and everyone calls you Joche (Hochee)?"

The boy nodded.

"Well, how about coming to work for me? I need a responsible fella your size to scare away the birds so they don't eat the crops. How about it?"

Joche gladly accepted. Don agreed to pay him the standard Honduran wage, the equivalent of 25 cents per day.

Don's conversations with his neighbors frequently included the reminder, "We'll start our school as soon as we can. The boys will go to school half a day and work half a day so they can learn good farming methods along with reading and writing, Also, we'll teach them how to live the way God wants them to live."

Men began to think about sending their sons. Boys started dreaming about attending classes and working at don Donaldo's farm school.

8

May and June rains fell about the same time Don and Twana began to prepare for their third baby. Dr. George Warner, president of World Gospel Mission, wrote that he would visit them soon.

"Maybe after he sees the farm and hears again what we have in mind he'll tell the board about the possibilities," Don suggested.

"I hope that'll help others catch the vision too."

Don took Dr. Warner on a horseback tour of the farm, explaining once more the dreams and goals they felt God had given them. Later, in Tegucigalpa, Dr. Warner met with the Honduras missionary staff, who told him, "Mr. and Mrs. Donald Hawk have been here more than a year and have shown courage and faith. We've carefully considered the matter with Brother Hawk, and we approve the general plan for a mission farm and school. We think this should be made a mission project, subject to the provision of funds. But in view of the other urgent needs of this field, we feel the farm project shouldn't be financed from regular mission receipts. On our behalf, please take this recommendation to the board."

At that meeting, the missionaries also asked Don and Twana to consider moving to El Hatillo (Ell a-TEA-yo) while they waited for the baby's birth. "We need Don to oversee the construction of the first permanent building at the Bible Institute," they said.

The Hawks agreed. They hired don Victoriano to care for the farm, and Arthur Schnasse agreed to oversee his work. In August Don and Twana moved to El Hatillo, six miles up the narrow, steep mountain trail above Tegucigalpa. Don worked vigorously each day, keeping warm in the high altitude and cool fall weather. Twana sewed for missionary Doris Vesper and looked for small, sunny clearings in the dense pine forest where she and the boys could sit or play. They all huddled around a small kerosene heater at night.

"Sure is a different temperature here than out at the farm," they often remarked.

On October 17, Don wrote to Dr. Warner. *Recently we have talked with the Vespers about the possibility of our being considered as regular missionaries under WGM and the present need for more missionaries here in the work that is started, rather than starting a new project.*

We have talked it over and prayed about it and feel that if we are appointed as missionaries we will be willing to serve wherever the Lord can use us best. We have offered these services because of the need for help among the missionaries, not because we're thinking of abandoning our farm school project. God has called us to that work and we feel it will work out in His time.

At last a letter arrived with news that the World Gospel Mission Board had accepted Don and Twana as full-fledged missionaries. *Now we must raise our personal support as well as money to buy the farm,* they wrote to their parents. *We'll return to the States as soon as we can after the baby comes.*

On November 7, Don proudly announced to the other missionaries, "We got our girl and we've named her Twana Jean."

Five weeks later, the Hawk family boarded a flight from Tegucigalpa, heading back to a country and to people they had not seen for nearly two years.

Don and Twana soon learned the Churches of Christ in Christian Union mission department and World Gospel

Mission had formed an agreement. Both organizations gave the Hawks permission to raise funds to purchase the farm.

As Don and Twana left the CCCU missionary building after making these arrangements, they met Burnis Bushong, a young missionary appointee. "We're ready to start raising funds for the farm," Don told him. "We're selling acres at seven dollars each."

Burnis reached into his back pocket. "Here, Don, let me be the first to buy an acre." He held out a five dollar bill and two ones.

Receipt No. 881 from the Circleville, Ohio, offices of the Churches of Christ in Christian Union, dated February 15, 1950, and designated "First Acre," confirmed the purchase. Long after, Burnis jokingly boasted, "I bought the acre where the house is located."

Don and Twana traveled to churches in many midwestern states, telling the story of God's call to Honduras, selling the farm acre by acre. One evening Twana said, "This is hard, Don. We've always been on the giving end, and now we're on the asking side of things."

Don agreed. "But on the other hand, we're not really asking for ourselves but for the work God has called us to do. It's a privilege for us to do that work and a privilege for others to be able to support the Lord's work." From then on they both felt at ease as they presented their needs for God's work in Honduras.

At a meeting in Georgia they finally met A.L. Luce.

Surprise in capital letters spread quickly across their faces. "You're the man in the rocking chair," Twana exclaimed.

Don stepped up and offered his right hand. "At the Chicago Evangelistic Institute the day we met with the World Gospel Mission Board the first time. We never did know your name. Even when we got your letters, we didn't know they came from *you*. All you've done for us sure has been a blessing to us and our work."

"I'm glad to hear what God's doing for you down there," said Mr. Luce. "I want to help you all I can. When you get ready to build some buildings for the school, let me know." A generous supporter the rest of his life, A.L. Luce set an enduring example for his family, who continued the support.

As 1950 drew to a close, friends and family members who had originally expressed skepticism, said to Don and Twana, "We believe the young men and boys in Honduras are your responsibility."

The young missionaries calculated the pledges of personal support money and counted the cash they had received, then bought a new Jeep pickup. Don loaded it with a small sugar mill, a wood range, and as many other items as he could squeeze in.

"I'll drive down to Honduras," he said. Good friends, Reverend Don Humble and Reverend Earl Newton, announced their intentions to go along and help. Twana said she and the children would ride with them as far as Mexico City, then fly to Tegucigalpa.

A few weeks later they met again in the capital city. The men told tales of nearly impassable roads, few bridges, an unexpected train ride, and communication problems due to limited Spanish. "I wouldn't have missed that trip for a million dollars," Don declared. "On the other hand I wouldn't take a million dollars to do it again."

He did, however, drive that trip again. Sixteen more times he traveled overland, transporting equipment, supplies, family, animals, and vehicles into Honduras.

Neighbors welcomed them and once again Don assured them, "We'll start the school as soon as we can."

Twana laughed one evening as she said, "I'd know we were back in Honduras even if I had my eyes closed. I just stepped on a beetle and it crunched."

After several months, someone wrote to ask about the Hawk children and their daily activities. Twana replied, *Teddy is taking the Calvert School course and I am his teacher. He loves to go with his father around the farm. Swimming in the river is a favorite pastime, also, along with riding his red bicycle and memorizing Bible verses in Spanish.*

Timmy also likes to go around the farm with his Daddy. When he can slip away without me noticing, he carries a machete and cuts brush with it. Of course he's too young to carry that long knife, but he likes to, anyway. He plays with a lasso, and usually his little sister or the dogs are his victims. He would rather have tortillas than ice cream, though Teddy prefers the ice cream.

Jeannie is a cheerful two-and-a-half-year-old who always carries a doll or a puppy nearly everywhere she goes. She loves books and does her best to enter into games with her brothers. Beginning to talk now, she speaks more Spanish than English.

For Don, clearing, planting, and harvesting moved in proper cycle with dry weather and rains. He dreamed and planned how to create more living space. "We'll need it when we open the school."

Arthur and Irene Schnasse offered their house in Catacamas. "You can live here in town while you remodel the farmhouse."

The Hawks accepted the offer. For the next year they lived in the adobe brick house one block east and two blocks north of the city plaza, where a big ceiba (SAYba) tree stood like a centerpiece. Primitive Catacamas had no electricity and few gas-powered vehicles. Cobblestone streets on the north and east sides of the Hawks' temporary residence exaggerated the clomping of galloping horses, as well as the squeaks and rattles of carts pulled by plodding oxen.

The Hawks heard fights and shouts from the bar across the street and even gun shots near their door. Most men wore pistols at their sides and carried machetes, using either or both without hesitation when disagreements arose.

The day a man showed up and offered for sale a large black spider monkey, Don said, "Yes," and right away the Hawks named him Paco. Twana discovered immediately he hosted an infestation of lice on his tummy, back, and legs. "Oh shoot! We've got to get rid of that mess."

Don leashed Paco to the clothesline pole and draped him over the wire. Twana thoroughly doused Paco with bug spray, and while it did the job Teddy observed, "It looks like snow falling off him."

When Paco stood on his back legs, he looked Twana directly in the eyes. "He's so big," she protested. At first the monkey enjoyed freedom to roam as he pleased.

At the back of the house, the big courtyard enclosed within the high wall made a pleasant shady and safe place where the children played. Paco and the family dog resided there too. Once when Twana baked rolls and set them inside the screened porch to cool, she watched Paco open the screen door, take two rolls, sneak back outside, give one to the dog, and eat the other himself.

Reporting this to Don, Twana said, "That monkey's just too smart." As Paco grew older, Twana found more than one occasion to make the same accusation.

The courtyard provided an ideal setting for Sunday school. Twana invited children who lived nearby to come each week to sing with her and to hear a Bible story.

"I like to come here," seven-year-old José Hernandez said one Sunday. "But my grandmother does not like me to come. She gets upset. I must not stay long today."

Living in town, Twana did her own buying instead of sending a list with Don. A five-minute stroll with the children tagging behind took her to doña Chocha's well-stocked shop. Dignified and petite, the Honduran shopkeeper showed fabrics, buttons, thread, lace, and ribbons that always attracted Twana. Doña Chocha's neatly arranged shelves also held household and personal items, dishes, and hardware.

Leisurely looking while Twana made decisions, Don suddenly spoke with new enthusiasm. "Twana, do you see what I see up on that shelf?"

"Firecrackers! I might have known you would find them."

"Boy, am I glad to know we can get 'em here."

For years to come, anyone visiting the farm soon learned they could expect a sudden BANG anytime, day or night.

Don and Twana formed a lasting friendship with doña Chocha and her husband. Children from the two families had good times together also. Many years later, doña Chocha, retired by that time, said, "We were always impressed with the Hawk children."

That year Don bought an old truck. "Now we can haul timber in from the mountains to our sawmill," he said. "It's taking a lot of lumber to remodel our house. I'm going to inquire around Teguc and see if anyone knows a truck driver I can hire."

Next trip in, someone recommended a driver, saying, "He's driven some for others, and he knows how to manage the mountainous curves and roads without bridges."

Don located the driver and asked his name.

"Just call me Ratón," the little man, barely five feet tall, replied.

"But that means *rat*."

Ratón nodded.

Later Don said, "I suppose he got that nickname because he's such an agile little fella."

Don continued the questioning. "Can you drive without brakes?"

"Si, señor."

"Good. I guess that's the main requirement for truck drivers in Honduras. Vehicle brakes don't hold up here." Don described the job and invited Ratón to drive for him.

Ratón agreed and moved to El Sembrador, bunking with the hired men. Everyone liked this truck driver, a friendly fellow and an orphan, who had grown up on the capital city streets.

At the beginning of Holy Week Ratón asked, "May I have permission to leave for a few days."

Don frowned. "You know what it's like this week. It's a holiday and there'll be a lot of drunkenness. I'm afraid you'll get mixed up in something. I think you had better stay here."

"Oh, no, señor, I won't drink and I won't take part in fights."

"I wish you wouldn't go now. We'll give you time off some other week."

"Please, don Donaldo. I give you my promise."

"Well, Ratón, I can't keep you here if you're determined to go."

The next day Don heard sad news. "Your truck driver, Ratón, was in a bad truck accident. Everyone except him escaped injury. He's in the government hospital."

9

"**I**'d better go right in to Teguc to see Ratón," Don said. "He doesn't have anyone else but us."

When Ratón saw Don, he moaned, "Oh, señor. My back is broken. The doctors say there is no chance I will ever walk again."

Don consoled his driver and assured him, "I'll come to visit you every chance I get." He kept that promise, giving Ratón a Bible and Christian literature.

Later, Don heard how Ratón grabbed the steering wheel when the driver lost all nerve as the truck headed over a steep cliff. Ratón guided the truck to the other side of the road and stopped it against the mountainside.

"You ended up as the hero of that accident," Don told him.

Besides trips to Tegucigalpa, Don traveled to Zamarano where he bought seed and hogs at the Pan American School of Agriculture. There, he met Melvin Eberhard, a tall, thin young American, head of the livestock department.

"I really like Honduras," Mel told Don. "I'm thinking about leaving the school and looking for property so I can farm on my own."

"Why don't you come visit us?" Don suggested.

Mel accepted the invitation and liked what he saw in the beautiful Olancho valley. He found it easy to say *yes* to Don's plan for them to work together. When the Pan American School finished that March, Mel, soon known to the Honduran workers as don Arturo, entered into this partnership.

That year drought begat desperation. Children cried. Mothers fretted. Fathers who carried concern for their children worried. Few Hondurans had enough to eat.

Unlike others, Don realized a good corn harvest, his first from the forty cleared and fertile acres along the river. Hunger almost caused a riot the first evening Don hauled a full trailer of corn into town. A small crowd stopped him beside the airstrip and bought half his load. To his surprise as he drove up the road toward home, he saw even more people flocked around the house, some trying to get inside. Don quickly recommended, "Twana, limit each person to just five ears."

The other half of his load emptied speedily. Twana sighed. "Their clamor for corn was more intense than women's struggle for nylons in the States during the war."

Don and Twana thanked God in the days to come that they could supply some of the people's needs until the rains began. *But we yearn much more to supply their spiritual needs,* they wrote in the World Gospel Mission magazine, *Call to Prayer.*

Besides the farm work, cutting trees, sawing wood, burning stumps or hacking down more carbon, Don helped workmen remodel the house. "We're sure thankful for A.L. Luce's generosity," he said. "He made it possible for us to do this remodeling."

They moved back to the farm in September.

Twana surveyed her flowers, grown now to lush proportions. *What would people in the States think if they could see these giant poinsettias, taller than I am?* Red, peach, and white hibiscus plants combined into a colorful patch that attracted butterflies of all sizes and colors, plain, striped, and spotted. Overhead, bright macaws and big-beaked toucans showed their colors regularly.

Red dust settled everywhere on dry days, and on rainy days red mud decorated shoes and floors. Twana groaned at the thought of red mud ground into her handsome rug as she once again spread it out. She swept the floors and dusted the furniture, then set up the customary bassinet before reorganizing their living space

"You can have this bedroom next to ours," she told Mel.

One night Don and Twana heard s*wish, bang! Swish, bang!* "What's going on?" Twana asked.

"Sounds like it's coming from Mel's room," Don said.

Mel soon showed up at their bedroom door with a badminton racquet in one hand and a large bat in the other. "Sorry for the noise, but I didn't want this fella to share my room."

"That's a vampire bat," said Don. "I didn't know we had any like that here."

The men measured the intruder's wingspan. "Thirty-six inches," said Mel. "I wonder if this'll be my nightly sport?"

"I'm on my way into town," called Don as Twana gathered laundry off the line. She waved and smiled. "Okay. See you when you get back."

Overhead, Paco sat on a branch taking great care with his grooming. Twana stuffed a final bunch of towels onto the already heaping load of clothes, picked up the basket, and turned toward the house. Quick as a pebble out of a slingshot, Paco leaped onto the porch roof. He leaned over the edge, daring Twana to go into the house.

She hesitated, setting the basket down by the porch. Disgusted that a monkey had the upper hand, she finally dashed inside. Glancing back, she fumed, "Oh shoot! Look what that monkey's done. He's scattered my clean laundry all over the porch."

January 16, 1953
Dear folks,
It seems I hardly am finding time to breathe these days. As soon as I got home there were beans to can, and I made jelly with the blackberries we bought in Teguc. Now the peas are getting ripe, and I am trying to give school to Ted and Tim. The baby had a

*touch of a cold and was fussy for a few days. Otherwise he is grow-
ing like a weed.*

Baby Terry, born in the capital city January 3, had immediately delighted his family. Local Hondurans vied for holding
privileges when he made his first public appearance at a
church fiesta held at the farm.

Twana's letter continued. *We feel the Lord would have the
school start this year, since the money has come in to finish the
house and some five dollar shares are coming in for the school
boys' expenses. If all goes well in the missionaries' annual conference, we ought to get a teacher from out of that group. Pray that
we will be allowed a teacher and that we will get a desirable group
of boys the first year.*

The missionaries did promise a teacher for the new school,
saying, "We would like you to develop a program for Bible
school candidates so they can finish their primary work before
they go on for Bible training."

"Well," Don replied slowly. "If that's what's needed, we'll
cooperate, but that's different than we had planned."

That same month Don traveled to Juticalpa, Olancho valley's county seat, to register the farm papers with the proper
authorities. Buying the farm from don Pedro Morales meant
owning the buildings and animals, but not the land. All the
land in Honduras, except those parcels for which individuals
held Dominio Pleno (DoeMINNyo PLAYno), belonged to the
government. Most other farmers hoped someday they too
could receive from the government absolute title to the land
they worked.

The rice crop at the farm got off to a healthy start that
year, and Mel watched it anxiously, knowing he would receive
half the income at harvest time. He sometimes dreamed aloud
about the farm he would buy for himself once he had the rice
money. "I'll be up and gone from here then," he said.

Time after time black clouds gathered over the mountains
and everyone ran for cover before the rain hit. Time after time
rain poured along the fencerows, but none fell on the mission

farm. "It's been this way since last September," Don said. "I've never seen anything like it."

By the middle of June, Don and Twana, along with Mel and the Honduran workers, lengthened their daily work hours. "We want to be sure we're ready next month when school starts," they said.

Two students arrived. A few other boys around Catacamas promised they would enroll. Burnis Bushong, who, along with his wife, Thelma, and their three children, now lived in Juticalpa, lined up two or three more boys. Miss Leona Powell, the missionary teacher, said "I can't wait for our school to start."

Only a few days remained before the beginning of school when Don's right eye began to hurt. *I must have a piece of dirt in it,* he decided.

10

The more Don rubbed his eye, the worse it hurt. "Twana, the pain's almost unbearable." Soon he felt like screaming if even the slightest bit of light penetrated.

The first trip to the doctor in Tegucigalpa gave only temporary relief. At the second visit, the doctor said, "There's no one here in Honduras who can treat your eye. You must go either to a hospital in San Salvador or to the States as quickly as possible."

Don chose a doctor in Louisville, Kentucky. There he learned that harmful bacteria had fed on the malaria bacteria already in his body, causing a tropical ulcer on his eye. "Treatment will be a long drawn-out process," the doctor informed him.

Poor communication hindered the news getting to the farm. When Twana finally found out Don had gone, she and the children hastily prepared to go, also. "The school will have to wait," she said.

The following months Don suffered, nearly losing his life. At last, as friends prayed, his eye healed but without sight. Don learned to compensate for this handicap, and few people ever knew he saw out of his left eye only.

Now that Don felt better, he and Twana set out to raise additional money for equipment and farm expenses. Ted and Tim enjoyed their first experience in public school, fourth and first grades, while Jeannie and baby Terry still had freedom from studies.

The family returned to Honduras in January of the new year, 1954.

Mel reported on farm activities. "It's the strangest thing, Don. That beautiful rice crop proved worthless. It didn't produce an ounce of rice. So I'll stay on a little longer since we didn't get any income from that crop."

By then everyone involved had concluded God intended for the school to educate underprivileged boys as first thought. "We'll begin the school in May," Don announced.

Leona Powell moved back to the farm and organized the boys' schoolroom, the new screened porch on the north side of the house. The thirteen used desks Don had bought in Juticalpa fit fine, along with the teacher's desk. One of the men helped her tack up two chalkboards, and later Leona hung five pictures of Honduran national heroes. A world map, the Honduras flag, and the National Seal gave an official look to the classroom.

Carpenters finished building bunk beds for the students' sleeping room. "Daddy, can I trade my bed for one like that?" Ted asked.

"Me too, Daddy?" Tim echoed. "I like those beds."

As the anticipation grew, the farm residents welcomed Benjamin Rodriquez, who had come to help Leona. Talk at mealtimes revolved around the question, "What shall we name the school?" Suggestions brought discussions but no decisions. Then, Virginia Sapp, visiting from Tegucigalpa, heard someone singing, "The Sower," a popular Christian song.

"El Sembrador salio a sembrar, salio a sembrar, salio a sembrar. El Sembrador salio a sembrar la Santa Palabra de Dios."

Virginia hummed the tune and thought about the song's English equivalent. *The sower went out to sow, went out to sow, went out to sow. The sower went out to sow the Word of the Lord.*

"El Sembrador," she said. "How about naming the school *El Sembrador*? Wouldn't *The Sower* be an appropriate name?"

"The Sower! El Sembrador!" exclaimed Don. "That's exactly what we'll do here. Sow the seed of the Word of God and sow seeds for crops. Escuela El Sembrador. A perfect name."

His strong voice launched into the other five stanzas. "Some fell along the way...and the devil destroyed it." "Others fell amongst the rocks...and for lack of root, dried up." "Others fell amongst thorns and thistles...and produced no fruit." "Others fell on good ground...and produced a lot of fruit." "How about you, my friend,...in what kind of soil has the seed been planted in your life?"

As the song ended, two early-comers ran around the house, hollering and chasing. Three more boys, each carrying their simple belongings, walked from the clearing's west end toward the house.

Don set his coffee cup down and held Twana's suntanned hands as he looked her in the eye and said, "I see some more boys headed this way. School's about to begin."

1 9 5 4 – 1 9 6 0

1

"**O**h, señor!! Oh, oh, oh!!!" "Yi Yi Yi!!!"
Wiggling and twisting as Don's strong hands scrubbed them clean with sand, thirteen boys squealed and splashed Talgua River water over their bare brown bodies.

"That's better," said Don. "There's plenty of sand and water, so there'll be no reason for anyone to ever go to bed dirty."

Twana smiled at the boys as they returned, clean and less self-conscious, to the house. "Tomorrow I want you to line up an hour before breakfast." She showed them a gallon jar of thick, pink liquid. "This is worm medicine. I'll give you each a big spoonful tomorrow and then two days later another spoonful and two days after that, another."

Next morning, eleven first graders and two second graders stood around the dining table on the back porch. Joche, who already worked at the farm, and his two brothers, Cisto and Heriberto; Manuel, son of don Pedro Morales; Miguel; Santiago; Alejandro; Luciano; Segundo; Reinan; Santos; and two boys named José giggled and whispered nervously as Twana measured the dose for one boy, then two. The third boy squinched his face and gagged. Boys numbered four through thirteen did various versions of the same.

A Honduran lady hired as school cook prepared mountains of rice and beans as well as tortillas by the dozens each day. "What a sight those boys make lining up for their food," said Leona on Wednesday, the first week of school. "Each time I wonder how they could possibly eat all the food stacked on their plates, but there's never any leftovers."

Oatmeal for breakfast went down well. The meat and cheese at other meals along with oranges, bananas, and papayas, pleased the boys, ages ten to twenty-one.

"*Ensalada?*" Joche asked when Twana spooned a helping of lettuce salad onto his plate. He took a bite and shuddered. "I don't like it. I don't like *ensalada.*"

"Weeds."

"Rabbit food."

"It's good for you," Twana said. "You must eat it whether you like it or not."

She felt pleased a few weeks later to notice these same boys asking for second helpings of salad. Turnips proved more palatable when served raw. Cabbage in any form pleased everyone.

One noon the cook served thick, nourishing vegetable soup. Soon after everyone sat down Twana noticed a greenish wad on the floor. She looked closer, asked "Who spit out the okra?" and settled her gaze on the presumed culprit. He quickly pointed to his buddies on either side.

"Well, here's more okra," Twana said and ladled another helping onto the embarrassed boy's plate. "These vegetables are good for you."

Many years later, some of the boys, by then grown men, laughingly recalled their first introduction to these vegetables as well as others they also learned to like: lima beans, carrots, beets, eggplant, broccoli, green beans, swiss chard, Chinese cabbage, radishes, tomatoes, and kohlrabi.

Twana established rules for mealtime behavior. Sometimes she scolded the boys when the conversation turned into an uproar. As the year progressed, table deportment improved under her instruction. Gradually, the divided plates Twana had brought from the States broke. Every year after that, the boys furnished their own plates, cups, and spoons. If a student could not supply his own, he worked an extra hour or two to earn his utensils.

A month after school started, Don weighed the boys again. "They've all gained weight," he said. "Some of these guys have never known what it was like to have all the food they wanted."

"Before they came here, I expect most of 'em just got along by eating a lot of sugarcane or chatas," Leona replied. The banana-like fruit, chatas, and sugarcane that hastened tooth decay could make a tummy feel full, unable to hold more at regular mealtimes.

Twana and Maria washed the boys' clothes three times a week, the family laundry once each week. The sturdy Maytag wringer washer, powered by the Briggs and Stratton gas motor with a kick starter, stood under the bell tower. Hot November-to-May dry season sun quickly dried clothes pinned on lines strung close to the house. The wide porch made an acceptable drying place on wet season days, June to October.

Each boy had brought his best clothes as well as a blanket, but after a scrubbing or two Twana said, "There's not much left of these shirts and pants."

"People have given money to help the school get started," Don reminded, "so we'll buy clothes for the boys. They sure like the new straw hats we gave them to wear when they work in the fields."

The next Sunday morning when the missionaries saw thirteen boys in new overalls and shirts, clean necks and ears, and brushed teeth, Leona exclaimed, "I can't believe the change in just one week. Those daily trips to the river sure have made a difference."

Don had previously explained to the boys and their parents, "Since this is an evangelical school, we will not have work activities on Sundays." Establishing the regular Sunday schedule, the boys and the missionaries met together around the dining table for their first Sunday school class. They sang and learned a verse and heard a Bible story.

With years of experience teaching boys at the Gregg Street Church, Don continued as Sunday school teacher at El Sembrador. Even after becoming adults, these former students remembered that every three months Don gave a little party for boys who could say all their Bible verses. "He always served cake and pop," one man said. "Also, at the end of the year, don Donaldo gave a Bible to everyone who could say all the verses."

Sunday afternoons found Don with his sons and the schoolboys exploring or enjoying a rambunctious swim.

Everyone gathered in the dining room for a service Sunday evening and again Wednesday evening. Now and then Leona preached. On other occasions Don brought the message, often saying, "Someday it will be too late, so now's the time to get right with God."

Though the school did not ask the boys to pay tuition, it did require everyone to buy his own Bible and hymnbook. Those who had no money worked extra hours instead. After hearing certain hymns only a few times, the boys declared favorites, boisterously singing, "Master the Tempest Is Raging," "Onward Christian Soldiers," and "Soldiers of Emanuel."

Escuela El Sembrador functioned in an orderly manner, thanks to the big bell Don hauled to Honduras in 1950 and installed on the tower near the southeast corner of the house. The wake-up bell rang at 5:40 a.m., the lunch bell at 11:20, the work bell at 12:40, and the day's best-sounding bell at 4:40, reminding everyone that classes and work had ended. The bedtime bell rang at 8:10 each evening. In between bells, the boys enjoyed three wholesome, bountiful meals, worked half a day, and attended classes the other half. Recreation and homework meshed with everything else.

One morning only nine boys showed up for breakfast. During the night the missing four, including the only two second graders, had quietly left. No one ever knew for sure why they decided to go home instead of finishing the school year.

Leona and her helper, Benjamin Rodriguez, who had graduated from the sixth grade in Juticalpa the year before, taught classes held each morning. They soon realized only one or two boys had had more than a few days or weeks in school. With patience the two teachers helped their students learn the proper way to hold a pencil to write numbers, the alphabet, then their names. "I can't tell whether teachers or students feel the proudest of their accomplishments," Don observed.

Arithmetic and geometry, science, social studies, English, reading, and diction balanced with physical education, industrial arts, crafts, music, Bible, and agriculture. Monday to Thursday mornings Leona led a Bible study. On Friday morning the students saluted the flag, sang the national hymn, and did patriotic studies according to the plan for all Honduran schools. For grades, a "4" meant Very Good, "3" Good, and "2" Insufficient.

Every afternoon the boys worked in the fields or with the stock, learning and practicing different facets of farming. Don supervised all the work. He set the pace in the fields as he hoed the first row, demonstrating how-to. It could take several hours to hoe an acre of corn, unless the promise of a fun activity beckoned the hoe-ers forward. Don learned that "watched boys worked better."

Because of their size and strength, older boys received more responsibility and harder jobs. Don detected some hazards in assigning work to young, inexperienced hands the day one boy hoed out a row of beets and another of swiss chard.

Some students helped Twana and the Honduran cook, who lived with her two small boys in the native kitchen on the back porch. Boys assigned to grind corn for tortillas got up at two o'clock in the morning.

"We didn't have an alarm clock," one admitted long after these early risings. "We just always woke up in time."

Don, a former Scoutmaster and outdoor game enthusiast, readily coached the boys to play basketball, soccer, volleyball, and football. After a few practices, Don said to Mel, "This is all new to them." The boys soon caught on, however, and after meals the ball players' shouts and taunts echoed through the jungle.

The river's refreshing coolness beckoned the students for many happy leisure hours. The boys dove and swam and splashed with noisy pleasure as the water washed away not only the dirt and sweat, but also the cares of the moment.

Twana often noticed Manuel playing by himself, always with an airplane he had fashioned from sticks and wire. "I'm going to be a pilot someday," he bragged.

Privately Don and Twana concurred, "He probably won't ever really be a pilot."

Before breakfast one morning, Don set a bucket of milk on the kitchen table. "I just found out four of the bigger boys sneaked out after we all went to bed last night. They walked to a neighboring village fiesta."

"That's the first time that's happened. Are you going to talk to them?"

"Yes, right now."

He rounded up the guilty four who had silly grins. "Well, I think you know what I'm going to say."

Four dark heads nodded. "We only wanted to see what was going on," one ventured to explain.

Another added, "But don Donaldo, everything was closed up by the time we got there."

"We came right back here," said a third.

Don looked from one face to another. "You know sneaking away is against the rules. We've made these rules for your good. Sneaking off at night that way could get you into more trouble than just with me."

Four dark heads nodded again. One by one the boys said, "I'm sorry." Then they prayed, asking God to help them not do anything like that again.

The next day Don announced, "I'm going to take the schoolboys to town in the truck. However, you four who sneaked out the other night can't go. You'll have to stay at the farm and work. We don't like to have to punish you, but we love you boys, and part of loving you is to help you learn to do what's right."

He and Twana figured out different ways to deal with different personalities. For some, to lose playtime privileges, such as swimming, proved sufficient. Others needed stronger measures. Sitting beside a small open-ended tent-shaped shed shucking several hundred ears of corn gave a lawbreaker plenty of time to think about his misdeeds. Some boys responded well to walking back and forth several times from the house to the farm entrance, nearly a mile away. Later, when the student population had grown, Don sometimes made two fighters take turns carrying each other on their backs for a round-trip to the river. By the time they finished, the boys usually tumbled into a laughing heap, no longer at odds. Now and then Don insisted that fighters hug each other and apologize.

Clearing more land for crops never ceased. Trees the workers cut provided usable lumber for El Sembrador building projects. Planting and harvesting continued regularly. Besides corn, Don placed sugarcane, sweet potatoes, various vegetables, sorghum, chatas, castor beans, red beans, rice, and a small grain-like corn, maicillo (mySEEyo), under cultivation on the more than one hundred acres of cleared land. He already had tried sudan grass, soy beans, oats, and kaffir corn, all new to the district.

The crops did well. Don noted, "They're better than the average because they're in plowed ground. In fact, we'll plant some cotton soon."

Someone sent budding material to graft onto orange, grapefruit, and lemon trees Don had planted three years earlier. He and Twana looked forward to a good-sized citrus crop in five years, but until then they agreed, "Wild oranges make good juice."

Don organized a Hog Project, which before long earned cash to help with day-by-day expenses. These purebred hogs, in years to come, attracted ambitious thieves, who sneaked onto the farm at night with bread dipped in beer. "Drunk hogs don't squeal," Don admitted.

Twana's days began early and ended late. Along with laundry and cooking, she taught school lessons to Teddy and Timmy as well as helping Jeannie learn letters and numbers. The schoolboys sought her out to treat their bug and tick bites, scratches, smashed fingers, and simple cuts. Close living quarters helped colds and coughs make their rounds rapidly. In later years, she occasionally radioed for a Missionary Aviation Fellowship (MAF) plane to transport seriously ill or injured students to the hospital in Siquatepeque, north of Tegucigalpa.

As vegetables ripened in the garden, Twana canned and preserved so her family and the boys would always have plenty. A few nights after she sealed a batch of homemade root beer in canning jars, she called to Don from the bedroom, "My head aches. Would you please get me a drink of water so I can take an aspirin?"

He reached for a glass, then suddenly tensed.

Gunshots. Outside. More shots. Could there be a roving band of outlaws out there? Supposedly they've all disappeared, but maybe not.

Quickly he filled the glass and took it to Twana, who flopped backwards on the bed, laughing. "Did you hear that? It's the end of my root beer. All the lids just now exploded!"

On his occasional trips to Tegucigalpa, Don visited Ratón in the government hospital. The former driver, still unable to move his legs, welcomed Don and readily accepted the additional Christian literature he brought. "The nurses do not like it that I have these papers," he whispered.

Later, at El Sembrador, Don discussed Ratón's situation with Twana. "The nurses don't like his interest in our religion. If I can find a wheelchair for him, he would do fine out here,

I'm sure. His hands are okay, so he could keep our vehicles repaired."

A long time passed before this idea turned into reality.

The boys respected Don and Twana, recognizing their love and appreciating the disciplined life at El Sembrador. Farm work and studies kept everyone busy, but fun times eased the drudgery. Birthday celebrations every two or three months brought out colorful piñatas made of clay pots. Eager for the candy inside, the boys dived under the piñata before the hitter connected with it, showering candy everywhere.

Special foods, such as pasteles, also appeared for special occasions. These pastries, flat or rolled-up and yummy with brown or white sugar and raisins, reminded Twana of American sweetrolls. The boys also liked nacatamales, a cornmeal-and-broth dough, filled with chicken, potatoes, and rice, then wrapped in banana leaves and cooked.

Christmas that first school year set the pattern for Christmases thereafter. The missionaries delved into their storage barrels and made a little bag of gifts for each boy. New jeans, T-shirts, sox, underwear, handkerchiefs, combs, jacks, toothpaste, and toothbrushes brought white-teethed smiles that said as much as their words "Muchas gracias."

The program on December 22, the day after the gift-giving and receiving, gave the students their first opportunity to stand before their families who had come for the special occasion. The boys each recited a poem and together as a choir, sang Christmas hymns, choruses, and songs they had learned that school year. For the finale, adult workers from the farm joined them to dramatize the long-ago events at Bethlehem.

On Christmas Eve missionaries, staff, and boys who had not gone to their own homes gathered in the dining room for a good supper together. Squash cooked with brown sugar, nacatamales, fried beans, coffee, and Twana's homemade candies pleased everyone.

The Hawk family, Leona, and Mel, who had again announced plans to stay awhile longer, enjoyed dinner together the next day. A pine tree, brought from the mountains and later decorated, reminded them of American Christmas celebrations. "Warm weather at Christmas is different from what we were used to in Ohio," Twana pointed out. "The spirit's the same though."

In later years, World Gospel Mission missionaries from Tegucigalpa and elsewhere joined the festivities at El Sembrador. They had to make do, then, with big twigs someone sprayed silver and trimmed with ornaments since the missionaries no longer had permission to cut trees in the mountains.

The Hawks enjoyed get-togethers, Christmas and otherwise, that brought the outside world into their isolated existence. Don anticipated the right moment to light firecrackers outside under windows, beyond a group, or wherever he thought would take the most people by surprise. To this day former missionaries and other El Sembrador visitors laughingly recall times Don's playfulness made their hearts skip a few beats.

The missionary women rallied to help Twana with extra cooking. Art Vesper invariably asked, "Twana, did you make some of those good brownies? I like them better than anything." They took turns organizing the endless dishwashing and the constant job of boiling enough water for drinking and cooking. Everyone agreed, "Twana is a wonderful hostess. She never makes us feel we're in the way."

The children, especially those from the city, forever remembered the spacious area where they could roam and play. Adults relaxed and took time for games, inside and outside. Sometimes they discussed business relating to their tasks, and always they prayed together.

That first school year ripened along with the crops. The missionaries, who wanted to see every boy ready to carry out the Great Commission, thanked God most of the nine boys had accepted the Lord. "And they're showing good interest in spiritual things," Leona said.

Because the Honduran government had accredited the school, examiners appointed by the government arrived at El Sembrador on December 16 to give the same final exams they gave in other schools. Before this day, the boys reviewed anxiously. The teachers looked over past lessons to make sure they had not missed anything. Missionaries prayed. "If the boys make a good showing, it'll be a great encouragement to them," said Twana.

The examiners, two women Leona had known in Juticalpa, gave the exams and graded them. They presented their handwritten report:

1. *The teacher was Leona Powell with cooperation from Professor Benjamin Rodriquez. Benjamin taught the classes that Leona was unable to teach being she is a foreigner.*

2. *The final exam results are the following:*
   13 students registered
   9 students took the exam
   4 students did very good
   4 students did average
   1 student failed

3. *From what we could observe, the school is in good condition. The classroom is large enough, is well lighted and has good ventilation. There are screens on the windows.*

4. *The music class was taught by Twana Hawk. The agriculture class was done in the afternoon with 4 hours of practical work preparing ground for food production. Don Hawk taught this class. The students have learned how to use modern instruments for farming.*

5. *Leona Powell is the director of the school.*

6. *The furniture in the classroom is magnificent. They have desks for each student and they are in good condition.*

7. *They have an abundance of teaching material in the class-room.*

8. *We wish the best for this school. We see great hope in it. Congratulations to the director and all those who have cooperated with her on a great year.*

The Examiners

Leona showed Don and Twana the report. "I'm not surprised one boy failed. He came from a place where he had heard so many bad stories about evangelicals that at times he trembled with fear."

"But he came through with a real salvation experience about a month ago, didn't he?" Twana asked.

"Yes," Leona replied. "Since then he's been a different boy. He's taken an interest and really wants to learn to read, but it was too late to start this year."

She smiled, thinking about the boys dressed in their uniforms, blue jeans and white T-shirts, worn on Sundays and also on special occasions. "What a difference the Lord has made in their lives," she said. "Learning to read and write and to keep clean and neat has helped their morale as well as their opinion of themselves. It's been such a joy to work with them."

A visitor called El Sembrador "a well-run farm that gives evidence of the skill and aptitude of the Hawk family for such a ministry." The visitor went on to say, "Don and Twana Hawk have done a wonderful piece of work in getting it started thus far. They need our prayers and help."

Though finances had come in slowly that year, El Sembrador at last had a new shed to shelter their farm implements from the almost daily rains. At times the farm account stood at $0. Anxious for the day the farm would become self-supporting, Don and Twana prayed, curtailed the work to match the finances, and trusted God.

At the end of 1954, Don wrote, *There has been a lot of hard work and probably will be a lot more, but as we look at the boys and hear them sing, and as we look out across the farm, we feel that God is repaying us many times over for any little effort we have put forth. We are very grateful to those who have helped support these boys through this year. We are sure if our supporters could see the big difference in the boys, they would be more than glad to have made the sacrifice.*

Our biggest concern is finding adequate sleeping quarters. Many other boys have asked about coming next year. We hope to take twelve more.

2

"Here I am again," said Joche. His two younger brothers, Cisto and Heriberto, crowded around to complete their registration too. Others from the first year had already come to sign up for the second grade.

On February 15, 1955, Twana welcomed each boy as warmly as if he bore the Hawk name. When she saw José Hernandez from Catacamas, she took his hands in hers. He grinned as broadly as he did the Sundays he enjoyed Twana's Sunday school lessons in her Catacamas courtyard. "Don Donaldo told my mother this school is for boys like me. My mother liked that. She wants me to work and to study."

"We're so glad you're here." Twana finished recording José's information. She smiled at the next newcomer, whose mother stood with him. "Buenos dias, Señora Gonzales."

The mother's face brightened. "You remember my name, Señora Hawk."

"Yes, I do. You came here to El Sembrador to buy beans and rice for your family."

"And chatas, too. We were very hungry when we could not grow food, but your farm always had plenty of food to sell. I have brought my nine-year-old son to your school. His name is Ricardo."

"Welcome to El Sembrador, Ricardo. We're glad you're here."

Twana turned to the next boy standing beside don Pedro Morales. "And we're glad you came too."

Don Pedro smiled and replied, "This is my adopted son, Juan Morales. I told him this is the best school in the area."

Twana finished registering Juan, then showed the list to Leona. "Twenty-four students, all first and second graders. The nine who finished last year came back."

Leona pointed to one name. "I thought we'd heard his mother wasn't going to let him come this year."

"She wasn't, but he cried and insisted he was coming. So, here he is, and we could have taken in several others if we only had more room. We planned to take in twelve new boys and here we've got fifteen."

"It's too hard to say *no*," said Leona.

The two missionaries noted which boys had paid their tuition, the equivalent of two dollars and fifty cents. Those whose families could not afford that much could do extra work to earn their fees.

School got under way, but during the first week one boy left. "I miss my family too much," he admitted. Halfway through the second week, Don suggested that another boy leave. "He's entirely too small to be with the others in school and at work. He can't keep up with everything."

A few days later, Twana noticed a gaunt, dusty woman and two little boys trudging toward the house. She met them at the door.

"Please take my boys," the woman said.

"But school has started, and we already have as many as we can care for this year. Your boys will have to wait until next year."

The mother's haggard face sagged like a punctured balloon. She took a deep breath and told her story. "We've walked seven days to get here. Through rivers, even. My husband had an operation, and now he hardly has any stomach left. Before that, he heard about your school, and he wants to be sure our sons will be well taken care of. Can't you please take them, señora?"

Twana motioned for Don to join the conversation. Together they questioned the mother and talked to her sons. "They seem like worthy boys," said Don. "Let's accept 'em."

In spite of overcrowded conditions, classes and labor progressed smoothly. This year half the boys worked in the morning and attended classes in the afternoon. The other half attended school in the morning and worked afternoons.

Personalities quickly showed their traits. Some boys displayed mischievous ways in class. Another showed his bad temper. Don wrote in a magazine article, *All the boys need much prayer that they'll find Jesus as their own, and that they'll have a peace and assurance that will overcome all the superstitions of their early life.*

Parents who lived nearby often stopped to visit their sons at El Sembrador. Some also attended church services there. *We hope to reach them for Jesus too,* Don noted.

With Leona due to leave soon for furlough, Don invited Arcides (AreSEAdas) and Zoa Shaub Lemus (LAYmus) to join the farm staff. "I would like Zoa to be the school director and Arcides to help with the farm operation," he said.

Arcides, a light-skinned Honduran born in the western mountains, grew in his poor surroundings to become a tall, handsome man who stood straight, even to old age. Wearing his big straw hat at a slight tilt, he spoke proper Spanish, "in the aristocratic style," some said.

Years before, the young Arcides heard Arthur Schnasse preach a message from Revelation that convinced him to accept Christ. He quickly decided, "It doesn't matter where the Lord leads me, I just want to serve Him." This decision led Arcides to Tegucigalpa where he enrolled in the Friends Bible School and later fulfilled pastoral duties at a church. During this time he met Zoa Shaub, a missionary with World Gospel Mission.

Replying to Don's invitation, Zoa said tearfully, "We've been talking and praying about this. We didn't think, though, there would be any possibility we could go out there. We'll pray more about it to be sure it's God's will."

Soon they sent their acceptance. "My wife has a real call from God and so do I," said Arcides.

At the beginning of this new school year, Don and Twana welcomed Arcides and Zoa into their home, along with Mel, Leona, Benjamin Rodriquez, and the twenty-four schoolboys. The students and Benjamin crowded into bunk beds in the small southeast room. Lemuses moved into Leona's room, which she vacated since she would leave soon. Until then, at night she made the couch into a bed. Mel slept on the front porch.

Twelve people ate at Twana's table three times a day while the students continued to eat their meals on the back porch. "It's a good thing we have warm weather so everyone isn't cooped up inside all the time," Twana mentioned with a chuckle.

Student housing needs kept Don busy late at night drawing plans before construction began a few yards northeast of the house. Besides rooms for the boys, the dormitory would include an apartment for Arcides and Zoa.

Workers made adobe bricks and hauled rock for the foundation. "We'll step out in faith," Don said, ordering tile for the roof. This news interested A.L. Luce. He wrote on March 27:

Dear Donald,

Letter received. I've instructed son George to mail a check for $2,000. If you need more, let me know.

Construction, new crops, bigger gardens, more schoolboys, and lessons for the Hawk children filled every daylight hour. With Arcides driving tractor as well as overseeing other responsible duties, Don and Mel centered their efforts elsewhere.

"I know what it is to work," Arcides explained to Don one day while they drank coffee in Twana's kitchen. "I've only worked at village farming. Nothing as big as this."

"I'm so glad you and Zoa are here. We couldn't get along without you." Don filled his cup a second time. "You sure have a good way with the schoolboys. I watched you yesterday when you were hoeing out there with them. They really respond to your suggestions and help."

"They're a wonderful bunch," Arcides replied. "I enjoy 'em whether we're working or whether we're playing games together in the evening after everything else is done." He laughed. "Oh, but it does take a lot of patience to work with them."

A long time later a missionary commented, "I don't know who could have fit in better than Arcides. As a Honduran, he related to the boys in a special way we North Americans couldn't."

Arcides helped with worship services at the farm and later preached for evangelistic meetings. Zoa took part in meetings too, by preaching sometimes, playing the piano, the accordion, or the folding Estey pump organ. Trixie, her small brown and white dog, always sat attentively beside her on the piano bench.

As well as directing the school, she kept the farm books in a meticulous way. The schoolboys discovered quickly the benefits of working for doña Zoila, passing the word, "She gives us candy."

Tall with dark brown hair and a pleasant smile, Zoa taught music. She demonstrated to the boys exactly how to sing the Honduran National Hymn. "It's the duty of every Honduran over seven years old to know the chorus and all seven verses," she told them. Then she read the rules for singing the ponderous but beautifully tuneful National Hymn. "Stand up straight. Do not look at each other while you sing. Do not fix your clothes while you sing." She glanced at several who often tittered or giggled at the same time something serious happened. "Rule number 4 is 'Do not talk or laugh.' Number 5 says, 'Never whistle the tune.'"

Finally she advised, "Never clap after the National Hymn. Clapping is an unpardonable fault."

When visitors heard the El Sembrador students sing the National Hymn, they marveled. "We've never heard it sung so well and so respectfully." They noticed, also, how properly the boys saluted the flag, their right arms and hands placed perpendicular over the chest.

Hondurans welcomed Thursday, Friday, and Saturday before Easter as a holiday. "It'll be a holiday here at El Sembrador, too," Don said. "Let's take the boys to the Guayape (GwyAHpay) River on Thursday."

After finishing the morning chores, the schoolboys and some of the men who worked at the farm climbed into the trailer for the hour's trip eight miles south through the carbon and trees. Don drove the tractor with Teddy and Timmy standing alongside. Twana, Jeannie, and Terry rode with the others in the trailer.

"I hope these watermelons don't break open with all the jostling," said Twana. She, as much as anyone else, looked forward to this special treat. For some reason as yet undiagnosed, watermelons did not grow successfully on El Sembrador ground. This changed in years to come, and this delectable fruit eventually grew in abundance.

A wide sandy beach made a perfect place for swimming or just leisurely lolling around. Midafternoon, when everyone had filled up with watermelon, Don announced, "Come on. Time to go home." The hour's trip back to El Sembrador gave time for happy reminiscing about the holiday fun that soon became a tradition.

The next day, Good Friday, workers and students met together for a special worship service. On Saturday Twana and Zoa, with help from the Hawk children, hard-boiled eggs and then wrote the boys' names on them with a white crayon. "They look really pretty," Jeannie said later, when she surveyed the collection of dyed eggs.

Twana supervised hiding the eggs outside while the boys ate Easter breakfast. When they finished, she explained the surprise and told the boys to go outside. "Stand by the line we've drawn in the dirt," she said. At the signal the boys raced around the yard, peeking under bushes and pushing grass aside, eager to find their treasure. That became another every-year activity that pleased boys, who had never before experienced such festivities.

In later years, El Sembrador residents gathered early Easter morning for a sunrise service on a cleared knoll west of the house. Neighbors usually joined them there. A special Sunday school program followed, the boys singing and saying memorized parts.

Multiple activities rounded out days that quickly passed into weeks and months. The town barber set up business on the porch at El Sembrador now and then, the boys taking turns sitting on the bench. By day's end they all had a new clean-cut look. Don bought two good bull calves, one Jersey and one Guernsey, at the Pan American School of Agriculture. He learned how to make a living fence with mariado tree saplings that soon sported dainty pink blooms. Mel helped him organize their own version of a 4-H Club, which the students liked. The schoolboys found it quicker and easier to shell corn after Don rigged up a small motorized sheller.

For Twana as well as for Don, every daylight moment had to count. She hired local girls to help with her increased work load. Not all worked out successfully, and some stayed longer than others. Now, with Jeannie in the first grade, Twana's home school duties expanded. The children did well under their mother's teaching, and sometimes they finished a year's course in six months.

At Mother's insistence, the family ate together. Occasionally, as the evening beans and rice finished cooking, someone showed up to see Don. Twana always said to her hungry children, "We'll wait until Dad's ready." If the time dragged on, she sent Jeannie to Don, saying, "Now tell him in

English that supper's ready. We don't want to embarrass him in front of his visitor."

Most evenings, Don and Twana spent time with their children after supper. Twana often read an exciting book aloud or everyone played games together. Routinely, before the evening ended, one boy or another would yell out, "Come on, Dad, I'll wrestle ya down." For a long time Don had the upper hand in these wrestling matches. The day came, however, when the Hawk boys combined their muscle power and laughingly boasted, "See, Dad! You can't pin us down anymore."

Twana never knew what family pet she might find underfoot or overhead. Monkeys, macaws and parrots, skunks, exotic animals, including sloths and tigres, all had their turns.

"Mother, remember my *night* monkey?" Jeannie recalled one day as she drew pictures for her art lesson.

"The problem with him was that he truly was a night monkey. He slept all day and then wanted to play all night when you were supposed to sleep."

Piloto, named because he had arrived with the children on a flight from the city, Oscar, and Blacky barked themselves into a frenzy if a wild animal came too close to the cattle. Other dogs, before and after, also endeared themselves to family members.

At first, tiny Bambi had a special place in Don and Twana's bedroom. "He's too young to sleep outside," they agreed. Gradually he grew larger, and one morning the children asked, "Where's Bambi?"

Twana answered sternly, "Outside. Last night he tried to get in bed with us, so that's the end of him sleeping in OUR room. Those four little hooves are too sharp!"

The children rushed outside to find Bambi. When they carried him back inside, they asked, "Can you guess where we found him?"

"I suppose he's had a feast on some of my plants," answered Twana.

"Uh-huh," three voices chorused.

A deep sigh preceded "It's a wonder any of my flowers have a chance."

Six months into the year another famine brought hardship to Honduras. Once again people walked miles to buy corn and rice at El Sembrador. "I don't see how they make it," Don said. "Many of them have large families, and I know they don't have enough to eat to hardly keep them alive." He wrote to his folks, *Most of them get along on much less than the average American throws away.*

The schoolboys moved into the new dormitory in August, and Arcides and Zoa settled into the two-room apartment at the other end. Before long, El Sembrador residents told Mel goodbye. They all knew he chose to leave at that time because Wanda Sharpton, a World Gospel Mission missionary he had courted, left for her furlough in the States. "It's obvious he's head over heels in love," Don remarked. "I'm not quite sure where Mel is spiritually, but I believe we still need to pray for his salvation."

When Don and Twana received a letter from Mel a few weeks later, they praised the Lord. *Recently I prayed and asked Christ to be my Savior, and later in the week I was sanctified. Wanda and I will be married next June. We'll come back to El Sembrador as soon as we can after that.*

In December Don again brought Ratón back to live at El Sembrador. By then Twana realized she must also plan for another resident.

3

"I found this special wheelchair, Ratón," Don said. The little man's smile slowly widened as he inspected the unusual vehicle with an extension on the front to support his unbendable, paralyzed legs.

"Gracias, señor. Muchas gracias."

Continual pain often left Ratón unable to work. When he felt well, however, he and his young apprentices kept the farm equipment in good repair.

Don looked on with appreciation. "You're doing a fine job. Anything on wheels down here sure is a lot of work to keep going. Besides, it's good that you're teaching the boys some of the principles of mechanics."

Ratón no longer drank alcohol, but he still smoked. Don did his best to discourage this bad habit, and Ratón, out of respect for his friend and employer, did not smoke in his presence. Then one day, he became a new believer, a Christian.

He called Don to his room. "I would like to give you something." Ratón held out two large cartons of cigarettes. "A friend of mine from Tegucigalpa sent these to me, but I won't need them anymore. God has taken away my taste for smoking."

Don smiled and hugged Ratón. "Thank the Lord. We've been praying this would happen."

Ratón handed a piece of cardboard to Don. "Señor, I made a list of my sins."

Don read the list, then promised, "Since God has forgiven you, we'll burn this list along with the cigarettes. That'll be a wonderful example to the boys."

Later that day Don called the students to an open area by the dorm. He built a fire, then prayed. "Thank You, our heavenly Father, for Your love and grace that forgives a man and takes away his taste for smoking. We praise You for Ratón's new life in Christ. You've made him a new creature. Thank You so much. Amen."

Making sure all the boys had a good view, Don tossed the cardboard list and the cigarettes into the fire.

At the beginning of that school year, 1956, Twana wrote, *We have 34 enrolled. Their ages range from nine years to seventeen years. We have this big age difference in the first grade, but it doesn't matter to the boys. We have 8 in the first grade, 6 in the second, and 20 in the third.*

At first, we had discipline trouble, but some of the ones who caused the most trouble have been weeded out and then two dropped out. Those who are left realize they are to come under the rules of the school and are willing to do this for their education. Several of the older ones are beginning to show more interest in living clean lives. All the new ones are happy in their classes and really love to sing the choruses of the church services. Some have expressed their desire to become Christians. These boys need your prayers for their future lives. Only three of the new boys come from homes where there was any semblance of Christianity. Two are orphans, three are from homes with married parents, and the rest are from homes where most of them do not know their fathers.

She ended the letter with other facts about the harvest, *looks promising*, and their soon-to-come furlough.

That spring, Twana again readied the bassinet inside the house, while outside the men prepared the one hundred cleared acres for planting. The Luces offered $2,000 for an addition to the main school building, and construction began on the new classroom and sleeping quarters for the boys.

June 3, 7:30 p.m., marked the birth of Thomas Ray. On June 10, his father wrote, *He's getting real cute.*

Three months later, the newly wed Eberhards arrived at El Sembrador. Don oriented them and named Mel as farm director while the Hawk family, now seven instead of the four who had arrived eight years before, took time out for their furlough.

4

The Hawks returned to El Sembrador in November 1957, with five calves, three Holsteins, and two Herefords, "All registered," Don explained. "These calves are the beginning of what I figure will be an outstanding herd for El Sembrador." His plan developed exactly that way. El Sembrador cattle, both beef and dairy, became prizewinners of distinction, tempting scores of cattle thieves through the years.

He and Twana mingled with the students, and right away Don noticed Joche's absence. He hurried to the boy's house in the village to ask, "What happened, Joche? Why aren't you in school this year?"

"I came a day late and don Arturo said 'Rules are rules,' so I couldn't stay."

Don put his arm around the boy. "Well, don Arturo's right, but I think a lot of you. You've worked for us, and you did well in school, too. I want you to continue your studies. We'll welcome you back next year."

"Gracias, señor. I'll be there."

As Twana organized their household and put down the beige rug, only slightly stained and worn, she faced the end of one era, the beginning of another. She and Don reluctantly registered Ted, Tim, and Jeannie at a boarding school in Siquatepeque, a city several hours north of Tegucigalpa. "That's the best way for them to get a good education, but it'll sure leave a big hole in our family to have them gone several months each year."

When the family drove to Siguatepeque, Twana's dread grew greater along with the distance from home. *But this is the best thing for them*, she continually reminded herself. Everyone grew quiet as Don steered the 1957 Chevrolet station wagon off the highway, past the sign pointing up the hill to Las Americas, the boarding school for missionary children.

"Well, where do we go first?" Don wondered.

A petite woman bustled out of the nearest building and said pleasantly in a southern United States drawl, "Welcome to Las Americas. I'm Miss Beulah Burgess. You're the Howck family, I believe."

"Hawk!" Twana retorted. She frowned and sighed noticeably.

Miss Burgess's smile withered. "Oh, yes...Hawk. Of course. My mistake. Well, come on in."

Someday everyone could laugh about that unintentional mispronunciation, but on that somber day no smiles appeared.

Twana took a deep breath and blinked back tears. She grabbed Jeannie's suitcase. How could she even think of leaving three of her most precious possessions here? She swallowed hard and told herself, *Of course we've made the right decision. Everything will work out just fine. But how can I...*

Miss Burgess, enthusiastic and cheerful, said, "I'm the boys' dorm mother and a teacher as well. I'll show the children to their rooms. Let's see, Ted, you're in the eighth grade, and Tim's in the sixth. Jeannie, third?"

Everyone nodded, and the animated teacher/dorm mother motioned to Don and Twana. "You can tag along if you want."

The moment they had dreaded shoved itself upon them like an uninvited guest. "We'll come see you when we can," Twana promised, trying to make her voice sound normal.

"I'll be up this way on the plane sometimes," Don explained. "I'll probably have a chance to see you then. In the meantime..."

Hugs back and forth stifled more words before Don lifted Terry into his arms and Twana cuddled Tommy. They looked back, waved, blew kisses once again, and climbed into the two-tone brown and beige station wagon and headed home to face the changes.

Don and Twana watched Terry and Tommy playing together on the big swing Don had hung from the tall guanacaste tree. "They've really become good friends since the others are at school," Twana noted. "It's a good thing Las Americas has that rule about writing home every week."

She smiled as Don reached for her hand. "Since that first letter the kids have never given even a hint of homesickness."

They laughed together about Tim's news. *We play baseball for recess, and we also have cod liver oil for recess.*

During those days, Ratón's health deteriorated. "I don't know what to do for you," Don said. "I'm so sorry we don't have any way to relieve your pain. Probably we had better get you back to the hospital."

Ratón nodded, his face lined and grayish-brown.

Don realized before long that even the medical people could not help his friend. "I'm sure he doesn't have long to live," he told Twana. "I hate to see him there at the hospital where he doesn't know anyone. I think we should bring him back out here."

On Wednesday, April 30, the farm people understood that Ratón lay close to death. A local nurse, wife of a Catacamas pastor, came to El Sembrador on Thursday to do what she could for Ratón.

"We all know you are not going to live much longer," she told him. "Are you ready to die?"

"Yes, señora, I am ready to meet Jesus."

Ratón died Friday morning.

"This is the first Christian death here," Don reminded the missionaries as a dozen or more Hondurans paced around outside. "It's obvious everyone's curious."

Arcides explained, "They're waiting for you to put the body face down in a dark room. Non-Christian Hondurans don't give the dead person any light to find the way to the next world, and at a death they have even more fear of our religion. All the time they pray for the soul of the departed during the next nine days, they will burn candles, never letting the flames go out."

Don listened carefully, then said, "This is a new experience for us, but we want everything we do to be a witness to these people."

"We must hurry," Arcides reminded. "We'll have to bury him yet today. That's the law here because of the hot climate."

The men carried Ratón to the Hawks' front porch where Don and Mel shaved and dressed him. Afterward Mel took several neighbor men into town to dig the grave while he purchased a casket, an unlined wooden box, as well as fabric suitable for a lining.

The men hauled the casket back to El Sembrador for final preparation. The inquisitive crowd had grown, everyone wanting a firsthand view through the porch screen.

"Let's lay some Spanish moss in the bottom of the casket before we put the lining in," suggested Zoa. "That would make it look a lot softer." Twana and Zoa arranged the moss and helped tack the fabric into place before the men gently placed the body inside.

"Too bad this is the dry season," Twana said. "We hardly have any fresh flowers."

"That's okay," Zoa replied. "Hondurans make beautiful wreaths with plain paper and crepe paper, both." She promptly dispatched a worker to buy several coronas in Catacamas.

He returned empty-handed to report, "I could not find even one corona in town. There were two deaths the day before and everyone was sold out."

"I know how to make Kleenex tissue carnations," Zoa offered. "I'll make enough to mix in with river fern."

Seeing Zoa's creations and the potted plants arranged creatively, Twana commented, "It looks quite nice."

"Yes, it does," Don agreed. "And you know, from the time Ratón had me burn his list of sins and his cigarettes, he lived a victorious life for the Lord."

"Even as the pain got worse and worse," said Twana, "he continued to have a good testimony."

Word-of-mouth brought additional mourners for the simple service where Arcides preached a clear message aimed at non-Christians. He made sure they understood, "Jesus Christ is the light of the world. Only those who do not know him live in fear and darkness."

At day's end, Twana's thoughts turned to the next *first* for El Sembrador. *Hilario* (eLAreeoh) *and Maria still plan to go through with their wedding. They're going to get their license next week.*

5

Twana and Zoa entered into the wedding plans as eagerly as teenage girls planning a party. "There'll be two ceremonies," said Zoa. "A civil one at the courthouse in town, and then a religious one."

Twana reminded, "They want that one in the new church here on the farm, even if it isn't finished yet."

"With two ceremonies, Maria will need two dresses."

"This dress of mine," said Zoa to Maria, "will do fine for the ceremony in town, but Twana will need to make it over to fit you."

Maria smiled as if she had just won a special prize. She beamed even more when Zoa suggested, "My wedding dress will do okay for the church service if it's remodeled." When she held it up for examination, it looked as if marksmen had used it for target practice.

"Oh, shoot," said Twana. "Bugs have ruined it. Well, we'll have to do something else." She thought a moment, then asked, "Maria, if I buy material and make the dress, will you iron for me in payment."

"Si, doña Twana. Gracias."

The white waffle weave embossed cotton dress, frilly with nylon lace, pleased Maria. No matter that she and Hilario had already lived together for nine years and now had four children, this wedding meant everything to Maria.

Her mother felt less than happy about the doings, refusing to give her consent. "It's a Christian wedding," Maria explained. "That's why she won't have anything to do with it."

Planning the wedding supper, Twana suggested, "We'll need plenty of food. I'm sure everyone and his brother and his cousin will come." Wanda and Zoa helped make several cakes, and Zoa decorated the wedding cake. Maria made nacatamales and said she would supply the coffee.

The day before the wedding, Maria's niece appeared at Twana's door. "My grandmother sent me to ask you if you would let her use your oven to roast a turkey for the honored wedding guests." Twana agreed. She smiled to herself again later when Mother relented and helped Maria make the nacatamales, then attended both ceremonies as a witness.

Twana and Zoa fashioned the wedding bouquet that brought a wide smile to Maria's face when she saw the fragrant white blossoms and tiny purple strawflowers gathered into a paper doily nosegay. Wild fern and philodendron vines placed around a large red and white spotted leafy plant beautified the church's altar area. Wanda created the final touch, a wedding bell with pink and green crepe paper streamers. Twana wrote, *All in all, it was a rather pretty wedding.*

Every morning the radio brought El Sembrador into voice contact with other World Gospel Mission Honduras stations. Promptly at six o'clock Don heard the field director's voice in Tegucigalpa asking, "How's everything out your way in Olancho?"

Don replied, adding the day's needs, grocery list, and anything else they wanted sent on the next plane. If necessary they connected in the evening also.

At first, the radios operated on power supplied by car batteries. This primitive arrangement created crackles and sputters that criss-crossed with many loud "What's that? I can't hear you." Later, more sophisticated hookups improved the contacts.

Twana grew proficient with long-distance shopping. When Don flew or drove to Tegucigalpa she sent a list with him. At other times she ordered basic items from a grocery supplier at

La Ceiba on the north coast. Her order arrived by plane within a week.

The day she received *one box of toothpicks,* as ordered, she laughed and then exclaimed, "Oh shoot! I didn't mean a big box of toothpicks. I needed only one little box. Why, there's a whole gross in here. One-hundred and forty-four small boxes of toothpicks. Oh my!"

Always an excellent cook, Twana made sure to have plenty of her children's favorite foods when they came home for holidays.

"Mother, can we still have hamburgers and french fries for Saturday night supper?" Jeannie asked. "And doughnuts, too?"

"What about pancakes for Sunday breakfast?"

"I hope you have cornflakes on hand for Sunday night supper."

"Or popcorn with milk and sugar?"

Twana's happiness flourished. *Family routines still mean something.*

Ted, Tim, and Jeannie fit back into El Sembrador life as if they had never gone away. They got up early, along with everyone else, and joined the family for devotions. Don read from the Bible before they all knelt by their chairs and took turns praying. Repeating the Lord's Prayer ended their worship.

After breakfast Ted and Tim lined up with the schoolboys, receiving that day's job assignments. Twana's rule for Jeannie, *Don't mingle with the schoolboys*, still held, so she helped with the laundry, or accompanied her mother to town, perhaps visiting neighbors on the way to or from. The Hawk family library offered books aplenty for Jeannie, an avid reader.

Thinking ahead to the next school year, Don and Twana decided Ted would stay home and do his ninth grade studies with Twana. Terry, ready for the first grade, prepared to go with Tim and Jeannie to Las Americas.

"Will you come visit us again?" Jeannie wanted to know.

"Yes," Twana promised.

"And send us special treats like you did last year?" Tim asked.

Again their mother nodded.

"The kids all liked the marshmallow creme you made for us." Jeannie licked her lips at the remembrance.

"And also the cookies and the brownies," the boys boasted.

Jeannie frowned. "But when Dad comes I hope he won't start another baseball game on Sunday."

"Was that a problem?" Don asked.

Ted quickly answered, "Sort of, but Miss Burgess said it was okay. We kids all had fun playing baseball that Sunday afternoon when you got up a game, but after you left one of the other teachers said we should tell you that Sunday isn't a day to play sports and next time you came you shouldn't organize a ball game."

"Remember the baby ducks you sent up on the plane one time?" Jeannie questioned. "We loved 'em a lot, but we couldn't have our own private pets, so everyone adopted the ducks."

On Sunday, January 25, 1959, Twana took Tim, Jeannie, and Terry to Catacamas to board the small Mission Aviation Fellowship plane. She told Don when he returned from Tegucigalpa, "Terry looked so little and bewildered."

Don kissed Twana and put his arm around her. "Terry'll be just fine, don't worry. He's in the same dorm with Tim, and he'll help Terry learn the ropes."

At El Sembrador the schoolboys arrived for the 1959 year on Monday, February 9. At the end of registration, Twana closed the book and turned her attention to a small, pathetic figure huddled under the big guanacaste tree. "What's the matter, Virgilio (Veer-HEE-lio)?"

He swiped his shirtsleeve across his eyes and nose. "I already miss my father. I know he brought me here so he wouldn't have to take care of me, but I miss him."

Virgilio took several ragged breaths. Twana put her arm around the slender shoulders. "Come on, Virgilio, I'll walk with you to your dorm room."

Several weeks into the school year, Don rushed to the kitchen. "Twana, can you please pour me a cup of coffee while I change shirts? One of the men in the village just came to tell me his son was murdered this morning. They want me to bring the body back to his home, but we can't move it until the authorities get there. I'll see if Ted can go with me."

Don finished the story while he swigged coffee. "These two men got drunk last night and ended up in a fight, going at each other with machetes. One man was killed, and his mother got cut up when she tried to protect her son. We may need to help her, too."

Don hurried off, leaving Twana to muse about Honduran life that sometimes dealt so much sorrow and hardship. An informant rode into the farmhouse yard after dark to ask, "Doña Twana, can you go help don Donaldo?"

Twana hurried to the victim's grass-thatched hut. Small candles flickered beside the dead man's body, creating distorted shadows that danced in the light of pitch-pine torches. The mother lay bleeding and bruised. Her groans mixed with staccato sobs made Twana shiver.

Don whispered to Twana, "They aren't going to do anything for the woman until they get the body buried, but we can go ahead and patch her up as best we can." While Twana helped him Don said, "When I got out to where the body was, I found they had built a little shelter to keep the sun off. José Ricardo, that's the dead man's son, sat there all day to keep the vultures and the hogs away. I'm going to see about him coming to El Sembrador. That would be the best place for him now that he's an orphan."

After the burial, Don spoke to José Ricardo Hernandez's grandfather. "Yes," the older man replied, "I think your farm school would be good for José."

6

"I like it here," José Ricardo said several days after he enrolled. "I know this is a good school because my Uncle Joche told me. My other uncles, Cisto and Heriberto, went to school here too."

Don made sure this small twelve-year-old newcomer had clothes and shoes he needed. When he knew José could handle work assignments, he said, "You can help Twana in the house." She showed him how to sweep the floor and dust the furniture. "I'll need you to help me with Tommy, too," she said. The times Twana drove the tractor in the fields, José often rode along with her.

José Ricardo stood on the sidelines as the bigger boys played ball games, watching every move. Soon they invited him to join their games. He also observed and listened with interest as the boys sang songs or repeated Scripture verses during Sunday school. "I've never heard about God before," he admitted. A few weeks later he received Jesus as his personal Savior.

José sometimes did not do his work properly. He soon realized don Arturo and don Arcides would discipline him. "Several times they've had to punish me," he told a friend.

More than thirty years later he said, "I might not even be living today if I hadn't come to this school and had the discipline I needed. Here I learned to fear the Lord. I also learned to work. I cannot erase from my mind all the kindness that I felt here. The Hawks helped take the place of my father."

On Sunday, November 28, 1959, the T-shaped Wright
Memorial Chapel, named in honor of the Indiana coal miner
who furnished the funds, gleamed with the early morning
sun's special attention. Twana, busy with breakfast preparations, reveled in the sight of the chapel that stood in the
cleared area a few yards west of her kitchen window. She
thought about the many hands that had carefully laid adobe
bricks for walls and tower, put in windows, finished the inside,
laid the red tile roof, and whitewashed the outside. Almost all
the materials, including the hand-polished mahogany pulpit,
had come from this Catacamas area. "What a blessing this
chapel's going to be to the school and to the community," Don
had said.

This special day, El Sembrador's first graduation, held
great promise, and already people had started to arrive by foot
or in ox carts. Frying another batch of pancakes, Twana
thought, *After breakfast I need to go over to the dorm and make
sure the graduates have their new clothes ready. They sure will
look handsome in those dark blue pants, long-sleeved blue shirts,
and matching ties.*

Two hours later, the chapel filled with joyful music sung by
more than five hundred people. Non-graduates, families,
friends, neighbors, farm workers, Honduran Holiness Church
pastors and delegates, as well as missionaries filled all available seats. Several people stood along the back wall.

Don sat directly behind the pulpit. Visiting dignitaries and
the graduates, who fidgeted and wiped damp hands along
their pant legs, sat on either side of him. Sweat beads glistened
on their foreheads. Smiles looked painted, unreal.

Twana sat on the right side, midway to the front, with the
schoolboys on the same side. First graders filled the front
benches with sixth graders near the back, others in between.
She lifted her eyes beyond the bouquets and elegant ferns that
lined the altar, looking fondly at the graduates, considering
each one *hers.* Some, she knew, already had future plans. One
boy promised to come back as a teacher's helper for the first

and second grades. Two applied to go to Bible school, and one would take exams in a few weeks, hoping to enter a school of mechanics. Another planned to live with a Christian family until old enough to go to Bible school. Her praise became petition as her eyes passed to the one whose family had discouraged him from following the Lord. *Maybe even yet he'll come back to the Lord and enter His work.*

The words Sembrando y Segando arched over the school's banner on the front wall brought tears to her eyes. *Yes, sowing and reaping, that's what we do here. We reap some now, some later.*

The Spanish words for El Sembrador's theme, *God, country, work*, printed as a triangle on the banner, had particular meaning for Twana that day. *Thank You, our Father, for Your presence in this place.*

After special music, recitations, and talks the boys received their graduation diplomas. Their faces relaxed, smiles became genuine.

Nearly as many people gathered the next day to dedicate the new chapel. Visitors there to attend the annual conferences for both the missionaries and the Honduran Holiness Church, remarked about the new kitchen and dining room, also used that week for the first time.

"We're grateful to Mr. Luce for the money to build it," Don said.

Early one morning after the busy weekend, Twana surveyed her empty back porch. Echoes from five years of boys' chatter and laughter drifted about like rays of sunshine. Their memories warmed her and she smiled. *Now the back porch will get its much needed rest.*

Christmas passed pleasantly, and a few days later Tim, Terry, and Jeannie headed back to school. Don left, also, taking an American visitor to see Honduran Holiness churches on the other side of the country. Twana kissed him goodbye, and wished she could see Ted. They had missed him, this first Christmas he had not celebrated with them. *At least he spent his Christmas vacation with relatives. I'm glad he's doing okay there in Ohio at Jeffersonville, but the family sure is dwindling fast. Tommy and I are here alone for a while.* She sighed. *Having the family separated is the hardest part about being missionaries. I don't like it, but it's just one of those things.*

At that moment her next baby squirmed, reminding his mother that before long she would have one more Hawklet in the nest.

When Don returned he told Twana, "There's a bunch of boys coming to school from up at Marcala (MarCALLah). I talked to Señor Padilla (PuhDEEyuh) and he's bringing them, but they'll be late for registration."

"This is the first time we've had students from the mountains there in the west."

"He's bringing about fifteen boys. That's including two of his own, Natanael and Nehemias."

Registration started and by the time the group from Marcala showed up, the student body had grown to eighty-three.

"How old are you, Natanael?" Don asked.

"Ten years old, señor. I am in the fifth grade. My brother is eight years old and in the third grade." He gripped his new wooden suitcase and explained as if someone had asked, "My uncle is a carpenter. He made these wooden suitcases for us."

A smiling Señor Padilla spoke up, "I have many financial pressures in raising my eight children, so I am happy my sons will be at your school. There is something, however, that causes me anxiety, Señor Hawk. You should know that my son, Natanael, always has a headache. It could hurt him if he has to work out in the sun."

"Don't worry, there's plenty of inside jobs. We'll see that he doesn't get too much sun."

That evening Don helped the students line up according to their height. "With the smallest at the front, Nehemias, it looks like you're number three." He sauntered along the wiggly line-up, numbering each boy. "Natanael, number twenty."

Reviewing the registration forms and calculating the size of their classes, the teachers thanked God that Edgardo Zapata had come to teach the sixth grade.

As Don strung wires for a new fence one morning the next week, a neighbor shouted, "Buenos dias, Señor Hawk," and ran to shake Don's hand.

"Buenos dias, Señor Gómez."

"Señor, I would like my son, Heriberto, to attend your school. Would that be possible?"

Don hooked the wire to the next little tree as he replied, "School has already started, and the classes are full." Conversation continued. At last Don said, "Well, señor, send Heriberto along, and we'll get him enrolled."

After he arrived at El Sembrador wearing his bright red boots, Heriberto stood quietly beside Twana as she recorded his information. *I should call him Red Boots,* she thought, chuckling to herself. She still remembered the boots thirty years later when Heriberto received official recognition as the initial pastor of the first Salvadoran Holiness Church, part of the first foreign mission field of the Honduran Holiness Church.

Early in March, Don and Twana boarded an MAF plane for the flight to Siquatepeque, where they signed in at the hospital. Tim, Jeannie, and Terry heard the news at Las Americas and rushed to see their folks after school.

"What will we name our new baby?" the children wondered.

"We'll need a name that begins with T," suggested Jeannie.

"Tony."

"Titus."

"Tammy."

"Tracy."

Tim, Terry, and Twana Jean looked at each other as pleased as if they had just found the lost treasure. "That's it! Tracy."

Later that day, March 4, they saw their new brother, David Tracy, for the first time.

While shadows darkened the mountains to the west, Don told Twana on a July afternoon, "Toño needs to go to Catacamas to get some medicine. Tommy wants to go along, and since it's time for Tracy to have his regular shots, I'll take him with us."

They left soon after, unaware of the excitement yet ahead.

7

"Okay, boys. We're finished in town," said Don. "In the Jeep you go, Tommy. Here, Toño, hold Tracy again." Don walked around the Jeep and slid under the steering wheel.

They passed the last houses on the right, the Catacamas airstrip on the left. Suddenly...*Oh no! I can't steer this thing...we're...we're...we're...*

The Jeep flipped onto its side. A frightened bird scolded and soared off to safer territory. Human cries and screams rose in its echo.

"Daddy!"

"El bebé? El bebé? Oh señor! Señor!"

Don saw Toño's empty arms, and fear created instant energy. He grabbed Tommy. *Where's Tracy? Oh! God, please help us find him.*

No baby boy sounds guided them in the near-dark search.

"Bebé? Bebé?" Toño called again and again.

Where is he? God, help us. Don prayed as he frantically scoured the brush and brambles.

All at once he saw the tiny form, a foreign object deep in the bushes. "He's here, Toño. We found him!" Don stood Tommy beside him and knelt to carefully lift Tracy into his arms.

The baby whimpered, his bloody head already nearly unrecognizable.

"Daddy? Is...is he dead?" Tommy whispered. "Is Tracy dead?"

"Not…not…no. But we must get help quickly. Let's go find don Remigio. He'll at least bandage him up. Let's walk back to town as fast as we can."

Nighttime sounds surrounded the three figures who hurried toward the town lighted only with flickering lanterns.

Later that night, once again back home, Don slammed the screen door behind him as he covered the kitchen in three giant steps. "We've got to get Tracy to the hospital as quick as we can in the morning." Tommy threw himself against his mother's knees, crying noisily.

Twana reached for Tommy, then gasped when her eyes focused on the still form in Don's arms. "Tracy's head! Oh, Don! What…?"

"Coming out of Catacamas the steering rod on the Jeep broke and I lost control." He handed the baby to Twana. "I did my best to keep us upright in the road, but the Jeep swerved and flipped over. Toño couldn't hold on to Tracy. I thought we'd never find him."

"Is he…is he…?" Tears fogged her eyes as she bent for a closer look at Tracy. "He's so quiet and his…his head's terribly swollen…he's still breathing. Do you think he's…is he unconscious?"

Don nodded. "He is now. He barely made a sound when I picked him up. He'd been thrown out about thirty feet into a bramble bush. On his head."

Tommy's sobs diminished into quivering sighs as he left his mother's knees and leaned into the comfort of his father's legs. Twana stood cemented to the floor as Don said, "Since it's Saturday night I knew there was no way we could get him to the hospital until tomorrow, so I thought of don Remigio. He's the nearest to a doctor we have. After he bandaged Tracy I got hold of don Pedro Morales, and he brought us back out here in his truck."

The news spread quickly around the farm. Missionaries and staff congregated to offer help and to pray throughout the night. Next morning, unusually quiet, gloomy-faced schoolboys filled the back porch or pushed each other for gawking space beneath windows. Don radioed Mission Aviation Fellowship in Siquatepeque.

"We'll get a plane right out there," the operator at the other end promised.

Twana's tired arms still held her motionless Tracy, whose head looked like a large mistreated ball. Only when they arrived at the hospital and met Dr. McKinney did Twana relinquish the baby. She and Don waited anxiously for the doctor's report.

After a time he hurried from the examining room, stripping off surgical gloves. "Tracy's head was almost like hamburger. In fact, I had to stitch inside his head before I could stitch the outside. By the time I finished, I counted fifty stitches. It looks like it'll have to be prayer that brings him through."

Four days later Dr. McKinney announced, "God has answered prayer. Tracy's going to be all right."

Don and Twana took their baby home the next day. "Thank the Lord Tracy has no permanent damage," they eagerly reported to the El Sembrador family.

1 9 6 0 — 1 9 7 4

1

In mid-1963, Don and Twana smiled at each other as they sauntered hand-in-hand toward their house, farm-fresh smells and night sounds pleasant to their senses. Tiny puddles of light from open dorm windows dotted the path. Tracy and his small white, long-haired dog, Osito, darted ahead, boy chasing dog then dog chasing boy.

Don squeezed Twana's hand. "I've been thinking about the change in people's attitudes since we first applied to the mission boards. Back then, nobody had ever heard of a missionary farmer, and that's why some people in the mission were so skeptical about us coming to Honduras."

"Besides, you weren't a preacher."

"Now most of those people are all for us and the farm school."

"A lot of that change happened when Dr. C. I. Armstrong...well, and others, too, made the effort to come see us. They got their eyes opened to our work and the possibilities out here."

Don kicked a small rock out of the path. "We have a lot to thank the Lord for. With the herds and the crops producing well now, I feel like we're closer to the farm being self-supporting."

For years to come that goal remained, but for a long time just out of reach.

The last three years had passed as if flying by on a SAHSA DC-3: thirty-six months, each one as full as Don's coffee cup at breakfast; for him, building—granaries, dorm rooms, fences, dams and ditches—clearing land, planting crops, cultivating fruit trees, developing herds, working new equipment and machinery; for Twana, cooking and sewing and encouraging new flowers into a symphony of color like she had admired at Puerto Cortes so long ago; for both of them, and for other missionaries and staff, too, more schoolboys to oversee and love and discipline, financial worries, and a new light plant; for the Hawk family, twelve months in America to renew friendships and support.

One morning the next week, Twana poured coffee for Don and sorted socks fresh off the line. She looked out the window and sighed. "Oh, shoot. Would you look at that? Oscar Pinto (PEEN-toe) just let the oxen walk all over the new trees I planted. That's the second time he's done that. What am I going to do with that boy?"

Her husband laughed and patted her shoulder. "Your plants always tempt the cows. I've reminded the boys to watch where they take 'em on the way to pasture."

"Well, I'll be glad when they take your advice. Oscar and his brother, Jorge (HOAR-hay), are quite the boys, aren't they? Did you see them last Saturday afternoon after they got back from hunting?"

"You mean when they made their own soup over a little fire?"

Twana nodded and folded a small pair of dark blue socks. "I don't know what all they had boiling in that can of water, but yesterday Jorge told me it was the best soup he ever ate."

"Probably armadillo or iguana meat. Maybe rabbit they got with their slingshots. Or they may have cooked up some edible snake. I'm glad we give 'em Saturday afternoons to do as they please. They need that change after working hard all week." Don helped himself to another cup of coffee and a piece of chocolate cake from the big baking pan on the table.

"That's not all they like about Saturdays," reminded Twana. "Those five pieces of candy we give each boy at noon are pretty important."

"In more ways than one." Don tipped his cup for the last drop of coffee. "It always amuses me to see how those guys use that candy as trading material. 'If you'll hoe doña Twana's garden for me I'll give you three pieces of my candy.'"

Twana smiled while her busy hands stacked the socks. "Also, Saturday's a good day because we give 'em cream for their rice and beans."

"Toña," Don said loudly enough for their house helper ironing in the other room to hear, "this sure is good cake. You can bake one like it every day, far as I'm concerned."

Pushing the socks to one side, Twana folded the towels. "Did you know Jorge Pinto isn't doing well in the third grade? He could get better grades if he tried harder."

"At least he's learning how to work outside," Don replied.

"He gets into a lot of mischief, too."

"He's part of the bunch that insists on taking oranges even after we've told them a dozen times not to."

"You'd think they would get tired of being disciplined every time they're caught. All those extra hours of work they've had to put in on Saturdays can't be much fun."

"Now Arcides tells me the milk boys are taking tangerines. He keeps smelling them in the barn, but he can't find 'em."

"Those rascals," said Twana. "Arcides has seen enough boys to know all their tricks, so he'll eventually find the tangerines."

Don savored the last bite of cake. "Our two new teachers are working out real well."

"I'm glad you asked Gumercindo and Roberto to stay on as teachers. I knew they'd be good, even if they aren't much older than some of the students."

By the time teenage Gumercindo Escobar's mother brought him to El Sembrador in 1961, he had attended three other schools. He wanted an education, and with his mother's encouragement he completed his fifth and sixth grades at the farm school, then readily accepted the invitation to teach second grade in 1963.

Roberto Acosta, the other new teacher, also arrived at El Sembrador in 1961 as a fourteen-year-old fifth grade orphan. After he graduated the next year, Don told him, "You've had high grades. We would like you to teach here." Roberto stayed to teach at El Sembrador the next fourteen years.

"It sure seems quiet around here," Arcides said after graduation in November 1963, when more than half the boys had gone home for vacation. He leaned his well-used machete against the fence and shifted his straw hat farther back on his head.

Don pulled out the big blue bandanna from his pocket and wiped his sweat-shiny face. "You're right. Too quiet. But the work goes on just the same, so I appreciate how the boys who don't go home pitch in and work twice as hard."

"Our boys are good boys. Even though I love 'em sometimes I wonder. I finally found where the milk boys hid the tangerines I smelled. Under the sawdust. I put a stop to that."

Don laughed. "That reminds me of the time Mel caught a boy with a block of sugar buried under the beans in his bucket. I understand Mel used the ruler to good advantage."

Arcides picked up his machete and the two good friends sauntered toward the rice spread out to dry on the floor of the big shed. Don knelt and scooped a handful of rice, letting it sift through his fingers. "The boys sure ate heartily at the graduation banquet, didn't they?"

Beginning in El Sembrador's early life, the banquet night belonged to the graduating sixth graders. The fifth graders started early that morning to energetically prepare the traditional event. After scrubbing the dining room with soap and water and hanging the decorations, they helped in the kitchen, their taste buds in high gear. The boys could barely wait for the baked pig stuffed with dressing, chicken, fried yucca, fruit salad called *tuti-fruti*, cabbage salad, and cake. That evening the sixth graders strutted into the dining room as if bearers followed with the crown jewels. Their everyday roommates, classmates, and fellow sports players, now transformed into servants, served the dinner, smug with knowing that next year *they* would enjoy the elevated status.

Don sifted another handful of rice. "Feels like it's drying just fine."

The inspection finished, they turned back toward the lane. "I saw don Saul Gómez here just before graduation," said Arcides.

Don picked up a sharp gray rock and hurled it into the bushes. "He came to check up on his nephew, Jorge Pinto. When he found out Jorge just barely passed, don Saul said, 'Jorge will repeat that grade.' That's why Jorge went around the next few days looking like he had bitten into six rotten oranges."

"Ah! I wondered. He usually has a big smile for everyone."

December's dry weather continued into January, registration time for the new school year.

"Look, here comes the teacher," some of the boys said, pointing to the tall young man as he stepped onto the porch.

When Don saw the newcomer, he declared enthusiastically, "Roque Caranza! You're finally here." He grasped Roque's right hand and turned to the boys. "He's not a teacher. He's going to be a student. Isn't that great?"

Surprise painted itself all over the younger faces. Several mouths began to whisper to one another.

Roque took a deep breath. "Maybe you don't want me here after all, don Donaldo. I'm big and tall and so much older than anyone else. I'm twenty-three years old, you know." He shuffled his feet. "I almost didn't come, but my friend Pedro's father said God was calling me here."

"Of course we want you. Last year when I saw you at the Bible school in Tegucigalpa you told me you wanted to come to school here, and I said we would be glad to have you."

"Si, señor, you did encourage me, but I don't have any clothes. Only these I have on." Roque unfolded the towel wrapped around his Bible, hymnbook, plate, cup, and spoon. "I don't have the required blanket, either, but I'll use this towel as my blanket."

"Don't worry. You can work extra hours to earn money for everything you need. We're just happy to have you." Don introduced Twana, saying, "She'll get you registered, and then I'll help you find your room."

Roque replied, "I'm so happy to be in a place where I can study."

At two o'clock Tuesday afternoon, February 11, the farm atmosphere unexpectedly shattered into a thousand fragments of sound.

Snarls. Screams. Shouts.

From his classroom in the church, don Edgardo Zapata ran toward the commotion. Students followed. A hired man raced out of the barn. Pinched-off words rose above the chaos.

"It's Tracy!"

"Osito's biting him! Osito's biting him!"

"Don Donaldo! Help! We need you!"

"Help! Doña Twana! Help!"

2

Sounds of disaster reached Twana at the Lemus house. Pulse pounding, she rushed across the yard.

"Tracy!" she screamed.

She grabbed him and whirled toward the house. Osito jumped to nip her arm. Twana sprinted, holding Tracy close. Blood quickly masked his face, dripping onto his brown shirt and smearing against her dress.

Oh, I wish Don was here...I wish he'd hurry back...oh, oh...what'll we do?

Behind her the shouts continued. "Osito! No! No! Run, boys! Get away from the dog."

Safely inside the kitchen, Twana held Tracy's head over the sink and turned the faucet to let cold water bathe his face. *Clear water...wash the wound...that's what we've read to do in case of rabies...*

At the sound of running feet, Twana looked over her shoulder. Don flung open the screen door. "Tracy..."

"They just told me. I'll radio MAF. We'll need a plane right away."

Twana adjusted the faucet again. Her mind brimmed with frightful thoughts while she waited to hear the radio reply. *Dog bites...rabies...nearly always fatal...*

"Over and out." Don stayed by the radio, reporting to Twana, "They'll get back to me as quick as they can. The pilots are all out on flights. Anyway the weather's bad across the mountains."

"What'll we do?" Twana asked. "Do you think...did Osito have rabies? If he did...but we didn't know."

Together they examined Tracy's head. He sobbed.

"Oh, Don, one ear's almost torn off."

"And the other's badly bitten. I think Arcides will have to shoot all the dogs. We can't take any chances."

The radio crackled into intelligible sounds. Don listened, then replied, "Yes, we did wash his face with clear water. We really need a miracle out here right now. Pray for us. Over and out."

Mel and Wanda, along with Zoa and new teachers Ramon and Delfia Turcios, gathered around in support. "The planes can't make it in time," Twana said. "Bad weather. Tracy needs rabies vaccine right away, but since that's not possible we're supposed to get some kind of antibiotic in Catacamas before we...before we...oh, my! We have to take him *overland* to Teguc."

Someone prayed audibly, and then, "Don, I'll make sure the pickup has enough gas."

"I'll pack food for you to take along."

"Don't worry about a thing here. We'll make sure everything gets taken care of."

"Let me get on the radio and contact Burnis Bushong in Teguc. He should know what's going on."

Zoa's nursing skills bolstered Twana as once more she gently washed Tracy's wounds with clear water. "I guess we've done all we can for now," she whispered.

Arcides entered to say, "The hired man cut off Osito's head when the dog lunged at him. I wrapped it in a sack and put it in the back of the pickup. The doctors'll have to see it to know for sure if he had rabies."

Don nodded. "Thanks."

Before they set out, Don and Twana knew Burnis had located vaccine in Tegucigalpa. "He's heading out right now," Mel reported. "He hopes to meet you halfway—in Guaymaca."

Long after dark, the Hawks and the hired man with them met Burnis in Guaymaca. "We came as quick as we could," Don explained. "We stopped in Catacamas and got an antibiotic shot for Tracy, but after that we had five flat tires."

Burnis prepared the syringe. "I figured something happened to delay you. With the good dirt road and the new all-weather bridges out your way I knew you should have been here a lot sooner. Anyway, now he's had that first shot, let's head out quickly."

They arrived at the hospital in Tegucigalpa soon after midnight.

An hour later, the doctor spoke his fears. "Señor and Señora Hawk, I'm sorry to say I give little hope for your son's life. There are three reasons I say that."

Don put his arm around Twana as the doctor continued. "First, he has bites on the head. More than thirty, in fact. He even has a bite in the back of his mouth. Second, the wounds are deep, and third, he is less than five years old."

The doctor frowned and looked more closely at Twana's right arm. "Looks like the dog bit you too, but your wounds aren't serious. Still, I advise you to take the anti-rabies shots. Unfortunately, we're out of serum. We're using all we had for Tracy, and I'm told there's no more in all of Honduras."

With a look that said "I'm sorry," the doctor returned to Tracy's room. Burnis motioned for Don and Twana to sit on the straight, cold, gray metal chairs arranged in a row against the wall. They sat. Don put his head in his hands. "Burnis, please notify the missionary prayer bands in America."

"I'll get a short-wave radio message to headquarters first thing when I get home," Burnis promised.

Many people in America and Honduras prayed. With phone calls to neighboring countries, the United States consul in Tegucigalpa located anti-rabies serum, and a cargo plane delivered it from Panama the next day.

Tracy recovered and all evidence of his wounds gradually disappeared.

Dried mud-prints on the center aisle of the church became airborne while ten-year-old David (DahVEED) Castro swept with a broom taller than himself. Twana gathered limp red flowers, leftovers from Sunday's bouquet. She looked up as she heard footsteps.

"Doña Twana," said Arcides. "I would like David to work in the dairy."

Red petals scattered as Twana met Arcides halfway down the side aisle. "No, I need him here to help me."

A short discussion followed with David acting as if he did not hear. Afterward he said, "Doña Twana, I thank you. I don't care to work in the dairy or the kitchen, either. I don't even want to cut with the machete like most of the boys do."

Twana patted David's shoulder and smiled as her memory replayed his first week at school. Don had told her, "I handed him a shovel, and he didn't know how to use it. He held it out in front of him and said, 'I can't use this shovel.' But I told him, 'You never say *I can't.* Instead, you say, *I'll try.*'"

Now, with the floor swept and dead flowers taken away, Twana said, "David, you've done well arranging the flowers the last few Sundays, so you can pick another bunch and arrange them for church next Sunday."

Early Sunday morning, Twana hurried to the empty chapel. One look at the altar brought hands to hips. *There aren't any flowers. David didn't obey.*

The boys filed in, and missionaries sat here and there among them. Zoa played a vigorous prelude, then Don's voice boomed, "No soldier can sit down. You must stand while we sing *Onward Christian Soldiers.*"

The enthusiastic student body popped up as if thorns had suddenly pricked them and launched into their favorite song. After singing all the verses, the boys listened respectfully to Arcides read Scripture, preach, and pray.

Twana eyed David when she heard the final *amen,* making sure to intercept him as he headed for the door. "I don't see the flowers I asked you to arrange for today. What happened?"

With head down and eyes focused on two ants scurrying along the floor, he replied. "I'm sorry doña Twana. I went swimming. I forgot."

"I'm sorry too, David. But you didn't obey me. Do you know what that means?"

"Sí."

Twana's left arm circled the boy's shoulder. "You must walk from here up to the main road and back five times."

"Sí, señora."

She watched him trudge west. After three west-to-east trips, Twana pardoned David. "I hope you will remember to obey next time."

As the dry season made way for June-to-October rains, Roque's happiness peeled away like tender skin from a festering sore. Finally he could stand it no longer. "I'm an adult living among young boys," he told Don. "Sometimes they call me names and throw shoes at me. I want a room of my own."

"I know it's hard," Don replied. "But, Roque, you can be a good example for those younger boys as you let your Christian light shine like the Bible says. Besides, we don't have space for you to have a room by yourself. Let's pray about it." Don put his arm across Roque's shoulders and prayed.

That night Roque slept, and the next day as usual he supervised the boys in the garden while at the same time working alongside. "Here, let me help you carry that sack to the cart," he insisted as three boys struggled with a sack full of cabbages as big as soccer balls. He looked directly into their faces and said, "I saw what you did yesterday. You peeled back the cabbage leaves and bit the tops off inside, then folded the leaves back into place so no one would know. I hope you didn't do that again today."

Jorge Pinto shook his head. "No, don Roque. We will not do that anymore."

By the close of 1964, "the most productive farm year so far," Don stated, he knew Roque would finish his course at El Sembrador.

A few weeks later at the beginning of the next school year, a neighbor man introduced his son and his nephew to Don and said, "I want them to go to school here."

Don's eyes and face smiled at the man, the ten-year-old son and the sixteen-year-old nephew, Cristobal (Crees-TOWball). "We already have as many boys as we can handle. I don't see how we can take even two more, but I'll talk it over with doña Twana and doña Zoila." The other teachers added their opinions, and all agreed, "Let's take the nephew. He's waited long enough to go to school. The younger one can come next year."

Cristobal, by Honduran standards a man at age sixteen, had no mother or father to help him. He had lived without adult interference most of his life. Quickly he found his place at El Sembrador, and because he wanted to learn and Zoa knew it, she reported after a few weeks, "He's doing fairly well, though he sometimes gets discouraged in class."

He began to attend the Friday night services sponsored by the young people's group. One Sunday night he stayed after the evening meeting to pray at the altar. Several older students and the missionary men prayed with him. A few Friday nights later Cristobal stood to tell everyone, "I have accepted Christ as my Savior. Please pray for me."

Don turned to Twana and whispered, "He'll give a good testimony when it's his turn to speak at his graduation."

Before twenty-four hours passed, the scene changed.

3

As from El Sembrador's beginning, the boys loved sports. Everyone vied for places on Don's teams. His long, muscular arms, when stretched out, successfully blocked any player hoping to dart past to toss the ball into the basket for a quick point. Don's football prowess awed newcomers, and all the boys admired and tried to imitate his well-placed kicks in a soccer game.

The night after Cristobal's first public testimony, Jorge informed soccer enthusiasts, "Don Donaldo can't play tonight. He and doña Twana have visitors. Soldiers. I know because I helped get everything ready."

"That's okay, we'll play anyway," someone said and kicked the scruffy ball. It quickly picked up momentum back and forth between players. Cristobal's right foot sent it speeding toward the goalie.

Suddenly he fell backwards as if someone had pulled the hard-packed dirt out from under him. His body landed like a brick.

"Cristo, get up!"

Cristo did not move.

"What's the matter?" an older boy asked. He and three others ran to see.

"Oh no! He's..."

"He's not breathing. He's dead!"

"Dead? Cristo's dead?"

Frantic yells bounced across the farm. "Don Donaldo! Don Donaldo!

143

Don sprinted out the door, Twana and their military guests a few steps behind.

Four big boys headed to the Hawks' house, Cristobal between them like a limp straw-stuffed scarecrow. They plunked him onto the porch. Don quickly straddled Cristobal. His able hands began the even rhythm of artificial respiration. *Push down...bad air out...release...good air in...push down...bad air out...release...* The two soldiers took their turns. Don eyed Cristobal intently, willing the sound of a gasp and the onset of skin-color pink.

Push down...bad air out...release...good air in... Dozens of pushes and releases assaulted Cristobal's motionless chest and ribs. Then, "You can stop now," Don said quietly. "We're not going to make him breathe. He's dead."

The sudden, rare silence that made time pause after Don's pronouncement left room for sounds otherwise barely notice-able: a distant moo, a bark across the river, and a fuss from a night bird on early rounds. Twana set time into motion again when she whispered, "He never complained about being sick."

Don wiped his eyes and blew his nose on a faded blue bandanna. "He's only been here two months. And just twenty-four hours ago he testified he had accepted Christ as his Savior."

"And asked for prayer, too."

After buying a plain hardwood coffin for the body, Don and Twana, accompanied by Arcides and Zoa, transported it to Cristobal's relatives in Juticalpa. They explained about Saturday night, and a cousin, who had witnessed everything, helped the family understand.

One member of the family said. "I knew he had some kind of heart trouble, but I guess no one else did."

"We didn't," said Don softly. "This is our first student death, but because someone was faithful to pray, we know Cristobal is in heaven today."

After the tragedy, Twana and Zoa organized the usual plans for Mother's Day, first introduced at El Sembrador by

Twana. Preparations for the annual recognition began long before the special day itself. Twana hoarded empty cans, one per boy, and filled them with dirt and flower seedlings. Each boy invited his mother or a stand-in to come for Mother's Day morning service. Excitement, like the blooms Twana carefully cultivated, blossomed amongst boys and their guests.

The students practiced songs and recitations. Twana and Zoa covered the gift cans with pretty wrapping paper tied with a twist of ribbon. They spaced the colorful gifts along the front of the platform with other flowers and plants at the sides.

Guests always arrived early on Mother's Day to fill the chapel, barely leaving enough space for the boys, their teachers, and the farm workers. Following the worship service, each boy proudly gave his gift, and more than one woman shed tears as she received a blooming flower done up so prettily. Afterward everyone gathered outside for punch, cake, and cheerful conversation.

Calendar pages replaced one another with breathtaking regularity. Plans for a new milk shed shaped up well, and new missionaries Tom and Ellen Dunbar arrived with their three small children. With furlough months in America looming ahead later that year, 1966, the Hawks kept at their work, summoning courage to face the challenges, thankful to God for His constant goodness.

Frisky, the gawky Dalmatian puppy Twana and Tracy brought home from Tegucigalpa the year before, had by this time grown into a sleek pet. Zoa included news about the farm's canine pack in a letter. *Frisky presented the world with ten lovely black and white pups last Thursday night, just a week after Princess had four. With Toby's five there are now nineteen puppies plus ten grown dogs on the farm.*

As usual, a few resident cats did their duty at rodent control, and in turn enjoyed fresh warm milk. Jungle creatures and birds had become less visible as farmhands cleared more land. The threat of snakes and a legion of unwanted insects continually kept humans alert. Every day's busyness, often tied together with humor, kept common anxieties at a tolerable level.

Twana sat at the table one morning to write letters. Her pen formed *Dear Mother and Dad,* then the screen door slammed. Laughter brought Don, with Frisky click-clacking across the tile floor behind him, sauntering in. He poured coffee and asked, "What's so funny?"

"I laugh every time I think about how my cakes disappear so fast."

Don sipped and puzzled. "Is that unusual? You know how I love cake."

"I know, but this is different. Just when I think there's enough left for supper, I look and the pan's empty. Finally I overheard Toña talking to Jorge and that solved the mystery. She said, 'Jorge, if you take this note to Roberto, I'll give you a piece of cake when you get back.' I'd say she must have sent a lot of notes lately."

Don's cup tilted dangerously as he guffawed. "I kind of thought she was sweet on Roberto. Oh, that's funny. Rewarding Jorge with cake. I suppose before long we'll hear that Roberto and Toña plan to get married. I hope if they do he'll want to stay on to teach."

By this time David Castro had turned into a dependable worker, worthy of special assignments. "David," said Don, "I'm going to let you drive the tractor and trailer into Catacamas to pick up a load of sawdust."

The young man's grin told the story, but as Don discovered later, not the entire story. He helped David hook the trailer to the tractor, then admonished, "You know where the lumberyard is, so I'll see you here when you get back."

David climbed up and settled on the tractor seat. He straightened his shoulders and with chin up turned his head slowly from one side to the other. *I hope the others see what job I have today.* The tractor started quickly under his practiced hand, and he put-putted down the lane toward the main road. Thoughts of a certain attractive girl in Catacamas brought an even wider smile. *What would she think if she could see me now? What would the town boys think if they knew I was a tractor driver? They've never driven a tractor because this is the only one around here.*

When David reached the road leading into town, he changed his mind about going directly to the lumberyard. Instead, he stopped beside the road to disconnect the trailer, intending to come back for it in a few minutes. Off he put-putted again, turning onto a side street where his friends could properly admire his skillfulness. He turned left at the next corner, and saw a totally unexpected sight.

Señor Donaldo Hawk suddenly looked four times taller than his actual five-foot-eleven inches. David slammed his foot onto the brake. The tractor jerked to a stop. Don took off his hat and waved it as he stepped out in front of El Sembrador's tractor. "Boy, what are you doing here without the trailer? This isn't the way to the lumberyard."

His face the color of a rain-spoiled strawberry, David's eyes investigated his shoes as he said, "Please, señor, I won't ever do this again."

"Remember, David, it takes time to gain someone's confidence. You can lose that confidence in just a moment."

Later, as an adult, David admitted, "I don't know that I ever pulled a trick like that again. Those things I learned then became part of my life. They've lived inside me forever."

That year, farm workers finished the twenty-stall milking shed. "Quite modern for this area," onlookers declared.

"Now," said Don, "if only we had the electricity we would see an even bigger improvement in our milking system."

"Improvement in the whole dairy setup, actually," don Arcides replied.

Time raced ahead, and as Don had predicted, Roberto and Toña married. Betty Padilla came for the first of three different stints as teacher or primary school director. Roque Caranza graduated, feeling so jubilant he set off firecrackers by the dozen, and soon moved on to study at the Bible school in

Tegucigalpa. "I've had a very clear call from God, and Tom Dunbar has encouraged me," he had told Don earlier.

Don and Twana headed to the United States for furlough, happy to be on hand for two important summer weddings. Tim married Sharon Davidson in July, and Ted married Joanne Watkins in August.

Back to El Sembrador in December, Don and Twana, Tom, and Tracy celebrated Christmas, and then registered students for the 1968 school year. "One hundred twenty boys," Zoa reported. "The most we've had yet." Tom and Tracy continued their schooling at Las Americas in Siquatepeque.

Natanael Padilla, the same Natanael whose height rated him number twenty in 1960 and whose father had explained about his son's headaches, returned as a trained teacher. "El Sembrador's a lot different now," he said after walking around the farm. "When I was here before we did everything by hand. Now the combine and the tractors help make the work easier and faster."

In July Tim and Sharon received appointments with World Gospel Mission for Bolivia, Ted and Joanne for Honduras. Twana Jean would soon graduate from Vennard College in Iowa, then enter nurses training in Duluth, Minnesota. Terry, a senior at Eastern Mennonite High School in Virginia, looked forward to Bible school and college.

Don and Twana welcomed news of former students whose names and faces they always remembered even when the number reached one hundred and beyond.

"I just saw don Pedro Morales and guess what he told me," said Don. "Manuel is a pilot now. For SAHSA. He learned to fly in the military."

"Really?" Manuel who filled every spare minute with stick and wire planes, appeared in Twana's mind as clearly as if he played outside the kitchen window at that moment. "Of course that's what he said he wanted to do, but none of us thought he would make it."

After the noon meal the next Saturday, the boys rushed from the dining room like cattle out of the chute. Don, hurrying back to the Hawk house, smiled. *Their favorite afternoon and not one minute to waste.* He heard loud laughs from a knot of boys near the guanacaste tree. *I wonder what those guys are up to. Jorge's there, I see.*

"Come on, Jorge," a high-pitched voice hollered as the Hawk screen door slammed shut behind Don. The others under the tree dashed like professional racers toward the river. "We already cut down the oranges and hid 'em," explained one runner to Jorge, whose tongue swiped across his lips, anxious for the sweet-tart orange he could never resist.

Another friend-in-crime explained, "They're down here by the river. Nobody but us'll ever find them."

The six originating mischief-makers stopped beside a leafy bush overhanging the water. Jorge crowded close to get his share as a fifth grader handed out oranges two by two.

"Oh, oh!" A fourth grader heard a noise behind them. He risked a look. "Now comes the old man."

"Quick! Get rid of the oranges."

"Throw 'em across the river so he won't see 'em."

Plop! Splash! Plop plop! Splash!

Horrified, the boys watched their bungled efforts float downstream.

"Come on up to the porch."

The culprits momentarily stood rooted, then with no particular signal slowly turned and headed back to the house. Don Arcides, straight and tall, walking with his usual stately gait, led the parade to the Hawks' porch, crowded with Saturday afternoon fun-makers.

Why did everyone have to be here right now? Jorge wondered, wishing he could suddenly turn invisible.

"Don Donaldo," Arcides reported, "here's what I found down by the river. They didn't expect me to come along and spoil the fun of eating oranges they took without permission."

Other students gathered around the seven. Everyone knew what lay ahead. "Jorge, you come first," said Don. "You're the oldest. That makes me think you're the leader of this bunch. You've heard the verse, 'Resist the devil and he will flee from you.' And here's another one. 'Draw nigh unto Me and I will draw nigh unto you.' Those are verses you need to remember. Everyday. Now, you seven boys go wait for me under the guanacaste tree while I get pencils and paper so you can write those verses over and over. Maybe that'll help you remember."

Years after that Saturday afternoon, Jorge said, "Now, whenever I preach from those texts, I can't help thinking of Don."

October 1968 brought news from Mel and Wanda Eberhard, working in Juticalpa since 1964. "Wanda's sick and unfortunately she's getting worse. We're going to the States to see what's causing the terrible pain." Sara Radebaugh, newer World Gospel Mission missionary, helped Mel and Wanda and their three boys get ready to leave. "We'll come back as soon as we can," they assured everyone.

October 25, 1968

Don was called at five to talk to the authorities about leads on the cattle thieves who have been stealing us and other farmers blind. He has been at this for the past three weeks, trying to get back the cattle, most of them of good stock he's built up over the years. He takes boys to harvest the corn crop, tries to collect money for jobs done, takes care of discipline, makes plans for the end of school, and receives people who come to talk about applications for the coming year. Before the day is over he will have fixed a tractor tire, a truck tire, and worked with the corn grinder. Don is administrator, counselor, disciplinarian, jack-of-all-trades.

The farm is now 1,500 acres. Prices are going up, but marketing prices are still low.

Twana

Four months later, Don developed severe chest pains. He and Twana heeded advice to spend several weeks in the United States. They rested and, as Twana explained, "learned how to deal with these 'ailments.'"

They arrived back at their Honduras home in time to oversee the summer planting, and just before life at El Sembrador rounded an unanticipated turn.

4

As the sun started its downward trek, the radio announcer blurted out, "Two enemy planes dropped bombs on Catacamas at five o'clock this afternoon."

Don jumped as if bombs had exploded beside his chair. "Twana, the radio just said Catacamas was bombed a while ago."

"Whaaaat?"

He spoke the announcement again.

"Bombs? Catacamas?"

"Honduras and El Salvador *are* at war with one another right now."

"I know. But, my goodness! I didn't have any idea something like this would happen. Was anybody hurt?"

"I don't know," Don replied, emptying the coffeepot into his blue enamel cup.

By the next morning, local authorities conferred with Don and then announced on the radio, "All Salvadorans, especially old people, women, and children should go to El Sembrador where they will be safe."

"That's a big responsibility for us," Don said. "We'll have a lot of folks here under our care."

Twana stared out the kitchen window as practical ideas took shape. "We'll need to figure out where everyone can sleep and what to do about meals, too. Zoa can help me get things organized."

As the hours passed, many Salvadoran men accompanied their women and children down the road, along the lane, and into the El Sembrador living area. Some arrived from as far away as Juticalpa.

Greetings and loud instructions echoed all around. Adding to the commotion, El Sembrador dogs barked and snarled as they guarded their territory. The farm took on a refugee camp atmosphere while people roamed here and there or huddled timidly alongside a building. Twana mingled amidst the Salvadorans, assigning sleeping arrangements on the church floor. Zoa dismissed school saying, "The boys won't be able to study with all this distraction." Don advised new arrivals, "If you're going to be sheltered here, you must attend our services."

The numbers grew daily as El Sembrador workers established a regular circuit around the farm to spot local hotbloods who might try to settle things themselves. Don and Arcides patrolled with the pickup at night, turning the headlights to high beam and rounding up refugees who had not yet sought protection.

Everyone helped with food preparation. Several men herded cows to El Sembrador and slaughtered them. Other local people brought corn, and the farm school shared its bounty. Women divided into groups, taking turns hurrying to and from the river where they washed the corn. A guard always walked with them.

Rain fell every day during the two weeks the Salvadorans camped at El Sembrador. Puddles and mud prevailed with canvas tarps providing little protection. Zoa circulated among the families, handing out medical supplies and observing, *A lot of these children have colds and bad coughs.*

The war actually lasted one hundred hours. Later, Hondurans and missionaries discussed the recent days.

"A scary time, for sure."

"Si. A very bad time."

"Wasn't it wonderful how everyone helped wherever they could?"

"Even the schoolboys worked willingly, bless their hearts."

"And to think, the only damage the bombs did when they fell on Catacamas was to kill one old hen."

The refugees slowly dispersed to their homes, and then the report spread throughout the Olancho district, "All Salvadorans must go back to their homeland."

Twana stirred the oatmeal before calling Tracy and Don to breakfast. They prayed, then sugared and creamed the cereal as they discussed this newest turn of events. "I wonder about Damian Gonzales and his wife," said Don. "They're Salvadorans, but their grandson, Rolando Alvarez, isn't because he was born here."

"More cereal, please," Tracy said.

Twana filled his dish again and Don passed it to Tracy. "I'm going to ride over and see what's happening with them."

When he returned he told Twana, who sat beside a basket half full of holey socks and torn shirts, "We're right. Señor Gonzales and his wife have to go back to El Salvador, and they can't take Rolando with them."

Twana's experienced fingers threaded a needle and quickly began the fine stitching to hide the hole in the heel of a brown sock. "What will they do with Rolando?"

Don cleared his throat. "They want to give him to us."

"Oh, my." Silence, then the question, "How old is he?"

"Seven."

"He's too young to come as a student."

"It would be okay for him to live in the dorm, though, and I imagine we could find enough to keep him busy."

Twana's needle wove more stitches across the hole. "He could go to classes and just listen, I suppose."

Soon they made their decision. "I'll go back over there tomorrow and find out when they want us to take Rolando," Don said.

Two Saturdays later, Don drove to the Gonzales home. Rolando sat on the ground beside the front door, his knees jack-knifed, his face buried between them, and his bony shoulders shaking with sobs.

"I...I...I don't want...to go with you, don Donaldo." Tears made dark dots on the dust.

Bending over, Don put his hand on the boy's shoulder. "I know."

"I want to...to stay with my abuelo and my abuela."

"Of course." Don squatted down beside Rolando. "And I'm so sorry everything is turning out this way."

Damian Gonzales appeared at the door, a sack clutched in his brown, callused hands. Tears wet his cheeks as he whispered, "Here's all he has."

Don stood and held his hands toward the sack. Señor Gonzales turned his eyes downward. He drew the sack close and twisted the top, first one way, then the other. Señora Gonzales, agony wrinkling her face, stepped from behind her husband. She focused her eyes onto Rolando while her fingers dabbed at overflowing tears.

Don swallowed noisily. All at once he felt as if a baseball had landed full speed in the middle of his stomach. His hands dropped to his sides as he promised, "We'll take good care of Rolando."

Time and words had no meaning as the silence swelled. Slowly Señor Gonzales offered the sack to Don, who grasped the meager belongings and helped the little boy to his feet. Instantly his grandmother folded her arms around him to hug as if never to let him go. At last she released him.

Don gathered Rolando, awash with tears, to him. To don Damian and his wife he vowed, "We'll do our best for him," and tenderly steered the boy toward the Jeep. "Let's go home, Rolando. Doña Twana's waiting for us."

5

All the way to El Sembrador, Rolando sat beside Don, his eyes pinched shut. Maybe if he did not see anything, he would not remember. Instead, his mind played back the days he and his grandmother had so recently spent at El Sembrador, sleeping side by side in the front corner of the church, hurrying to wash corn at the river, and sitting under a leaky tarp while they ate juicy slices of beef and warm tortillas.

Frisky's insistent barks brought Rolando back to the present. When don Donaldo stopped the Jeep, doña Twana reached out her arms to Rolando. "I'm glad you're here," she said. "You're back in time to eat supper with the boys, and then we'll go over to the church to see a movie."

That night Rolando sat on the church bench, feet not yet touching the floor, his eyes wide open and his mind busy. There on the front wall Jesus walked and talked. Other men Jesus called John and Matthew and Simon Peter moved along with Him.

Rolando liked what he saw. He also liked Sunday school the next day. "I've never been to a class like this before," he admitted. His opinion of Sunday school grew even brighter when the missionary handed him a picture and three crayons. "You may use these crayons to color this picture," she explained.

On school days Rolando visited the first grade class. Afterward he stayed close to doña Twana while she showed him how to help her with simple household or garden jobs.

Often, though, as he wondered, *What are my abuelo and abuela doing now?* loneliness showered over him like cold water.

Making sure none of the big boys had their eyes on him, he raced along the path to the river where he hid in the bushes and cried until the tears washed away his homesickness. He always made sure to show up at mealtimes, though, so nobody would ask, "Where were you, Rolando?"

After supper, doña Twana or don Donaldo walked him to the boys' dorm. "Buenas noches," they said. When the dorm grew quiet and dark, Rolando missed his grandfather and grandmother more than ever, but since he could not run to the river then, he pulled the blanket over his head to deaden the sound of his sobs.

Sometimes don Donaldo came to Rolando's room to say, "I see your pants are too tight now. Let's see if you can wear these instead." Once in a while he offered a new shirt. When Rolando's feet grew bigger than his shoes, don Donaldo always knew, giving him another pair.

Rolando smiled when he heard doña Twana tell someone, "I can trust Rolando, so I let him go in and out of our house like it's his own. And he's such a good listener at school I'm sure he'll know all the work by the time he's old enough to actually be a student."

Before long, when someone asked Rolando, "What's your name?" he usually replied, "Rolando Hawk."

Twenty-one graduates received their diplomas that year. "The most so far," Don pointed out to visitors. Almost before the sounds of celebration vanished on the wind, however, other news clouded the atmosphere.

"Over and out," Don said, and turned away from the radio to face Twana. "Wanda Eberhard died yesterday."

"Oh, no." Twana took a deep breath and sagged onto the nearest chair. "Poor Mel. We'll all sure miss her, but...oh, poor Mel and his boys."

Don sighed and said, "I'd better go notify the others."

The message Don and Twana received from Ted and Joanne three weeks after Wanda's death, restored their spirits. *Donald Harold arrived safely December 28.*

The first-time grandparents locked eyes. "Congratulations, Abuela," said Don as he hugged Twana.

"The same to you, Abuelo."

A few gray hairs among the black, Don's mustache now more salt than pepper, but they marveled, "it seems like only a little while ago Ted was born."

Mel and his sons returned in January, about the time plans for a hydroelectric plant moved beyond talk. "We could sure use twenty-four-hour electricity," missionaries and farm workers agreed, discussing the benefits of refrigeration and irrigation.

"With an irrigation system we could keep up most of the pasture land during the dry season," said Mel. "That would increase our milk production a lot during those months."

"And keep the cattle growing well," don Arcides affirmed.

They planned the system to begin at the river. Heading west and then south on El Sembrador property the ditch, placed at the high end of the property to allow for flood irrigation of the fields below, would eventually carry river water to a small lake, south of the main farmhouse. "We can stock the lake with fish," suggested Don. "That'll give us another source of protein for the boys."

Don asked El Sembrador neighbors for permission to take the ditch through their property. When they agreed, he promised, "We'll build a bridge over the ditch for you."

After he and Mel surveyed, Don obtained river rights. The government granted permission for El Sembrador to bring through customs a trailer loaded with pipes, equipment, the generator, and the turbine from the States. Don made endless trips into town for necessary legal work. At the end of one long day of business he remarked, "This project sure requires plenty of perseverance."

Twana patted his shoulder as she reminded, "And faith in One who can straighten out problems we never dreamed could exist."

Finally the construction began. Men with picks and shovels formed the crew that hacked and dug, foot by foot and sometimes only inch by inch to create the big ditch. More times than anyone could count afterward, Don or Arcides or one of their farmhands wiped sweat and either said aloud or thought to himself, "My! Such a big undertaking for ones who have such little knowledge."

Don enjoyed showing off the project. He tipped his baseball cap over his forehead to shade his eyes, pointed, and said, "There's where the small lake will form at the end of the ditch. We figure the ditch will be a little over three kilometers, and the dam there at the east end will hold the water. Below that, we'll build a small pump house for the generator that'll give us our electricity. Of course the ditch will irrigate over three hundred acres of pasture and crop land too."

"That's impressive," said one government visitor. "Señor Hawk, you've helped this whole area realize some new agricultural possibilities."

The farming now spread over two thousand acres, the cattle herd had grown to about nine hundred, including both dairy and beef. Artificial insemination had improved the strain, especially the dairy cows.

Representatives from the United States Agricultural Aid Program as well as other farm agencies pointed to El Sembrador. "Here's an example of what can be done," they said to Honduran farmers. "It's not impossible for *you* to achieve the same results."

The meat processing plant in Catacamas, managed by Don's good friend, Luis Oseguera, bought from seventy-five to one hundred beef animals each year. "We sure appreciate this sales outlet," Don told Luis. "It gives us a fairly good income to help with the overall costs of the school."

Sometime earlier, Don helped organize a local Cattle Ranchers' Association. He and Luis, also a member, often conferred. When he got home from visiting with Luis one day, Don told Twana, "I saw Manuel Morales in town a while ago."

"Is he still flying for SAHSA?"

"Uh-huh." Don washed his hands at the kitchen sink before helping himself to coffee and three big, chewy oatmeal cookies. "He asked if there was anything he could do for me, and I mentioned the belt we need for the combine but can't get out here. So, guess what? He's going to get it in Teguc, and when he's out this way with a flight he'll let us know ahead of time and just drop it out in the north pasture."

Twana shook her head and chuckled. "Well! That's a new wrinkle in our farm life." While she finished picking through the mound of raw rice, experienced hands flicking out small rocks, her mouth curved into a smile as she thought about the little boy whose boyhood dream had come true.

Laughter, whistles, and banter spilled through the open doors and windows. *Some sounds never change*, Twana thought. *If I close my eyes I can't tell if I'm hearing boys who've come and gone or if it's today's students outside.*

Faces and names from earlier times instantly paraded through her memory: Virgilio, finished now with the engineering course in Tegucigalpa...David Castro and Roque Caranza, enrolled in Bible school in the capital city...Joche Hernandez, employed at El Sembrador, married to Dora and raising a family...Gumercindo Escobar, finished with military service, working to save money for university studies...dozens of others, busy in their vocations, adjusting to wives and children, teaching and preaching in their churches.

She frowned as others came to mind. *Some still say no to God, like Jorge Pinto. Of course he prayed at the altar once when he was here in school, but the oranges were just too much for him. He couldn't resist temptation.*

Looking up as if these boys now grown into men all stood at attention before her, Twana said to herself, *Our boys. What a blessing they've all been to us. We've loved every one of them. Their hard work, prayers, tenderness, fun... And yes, Lord, even their mischievousness... Oh, thank You, Lord, for each one of them. For each one of our boys.*

6

As the student body changed, the Hawk family experienced revisions: Ted and Tim married, a grandson to brag about, Jeannie engaged to Dennis Johnson, and Tom along with Tracy in school at Siguatepeque. Terry had come home for the year while taking time off school. The parents welcomed letters and news from their children gone from the nest.

Las Americas Academy
Siguatepeque, Honduras
October 12, 1970
Dear Mom and Dad and the rest,
Thursday was the best day of school yet because I found a dead mouse by the wash-house. I wondered what to do with it so I put it in Aunt Charrolettes droor with his head sticking out. I put a book over his head and when she came in and lifted the book she saw the mouse's head and she jumped back and yelled she thought it was just a toy mouse and when I pulled it out she jumped back again because it was a real mouse. After we quieted down she said she might not make it through the year so please pray for her.
I got the money.
Love, Tracy

Jeannie wrote from nurse's training, *Today we started our new rotations. I am in surgery and I think I will really like it but it will require a lot of study. It is exciting enough to make me want to study, though. There are so many things we have to learn in such a short time that I wonder if I'll be able to do it.*

Tim and Sharon, finished with language study and expecting their first baby, planned an extended stay at El Sembrador on their way to Bolivia. Don and Twana looked forward to the time soon when Ted and Joanne would complete their language study and come to help.

Mel married Sara Radebaugh in September 1970, and they, along with the three boys, settled into the small home back of the Hawks' house. Farm duties claimed Mel's working hours and Sara practiced new skills as wife and mother. Later she assumed responsibility for the schoolboys' laundry, helped in the dining room, and filled in wherever she could.

As January 1971 faded into February, the proud Grandpa and Grandma Hawk told everyone about the birth of Tamra Jean to Tim and Sharon. Clusters of dainty purple orchids spilled off limbs of the big guanacaste tree, while tiny yellow and white flowers lay nearly hidden among that tree's branches and leaves. Mango trees put out yellow-green blooms that plagued some farm residents with allergies.

February's 28 days passed, roaring into March like a freight train rushing to stay on schedule. Workers busy at creating the new ditch persevered under a sun hot enough to broil a plucked chicken. Picks bounced off the hardened earth as if made of rubber. A bridge collapse set the process back. After Mel, the main surveyor, took a reading at one point, he shook his head. "Oh, oh. We've got the wrong level back there. We'll never get the proper water fall."

Workers retraced their efforts and tried again to dent the cement-like dirt. After he surveyed that section the next time, he called out encouragement, "Muy bueno."

Nearly twenty years later, during construction of a larger lake and hydro plant, surveyors declared, "The slope from start to finish is perfect as done the first time." Joe Luce, son of A. L., Hawks' longtime supporter and a prime help for both hydro projects said, "This confirms that God's hand was in the water project the whole time."

For the 1971 school year, recently-married Francisco Castro returned to El Sembrador to teach once again. His wife, Vilma, taught also. "When I came as a student in 1958," he told her, "it was mostly jungle all around the farm. In fact we hunted deer right down there where the barn is now."

"And you thought El Sembrador was the best school in the area."

"Si. It was. It had the best teaching and the best buildings. We studied hard and we worked hard. But Mama Twana and Papa Donaldo were like parents to me. Especially after my father was killed."

"I know how don Donaldo took you to your home that day and helped your mother with the burial and the details afterward, too."

"Si. He showed great kindness to my family." Francisco's mind reached into the past. "Don Donaldo taught me how to be punctual and how to be organized. That's helped me a lot with my teaching. In fact, I owe everything I am to the school. It gave me the hope I needed. After all, I was just a boy from a little village and from parents who couldn't read or write."

Vilma reached for a small black Bible. "I know you received this when you were a student."

"From our Sunday school teacher, don Donaldo." Francisco turned the Bible over in his hands and opened it carefully. "He was such an inspiration to me."

While the workers at El Sembrador pushed forward with the hydro project, locals fell in with outsiders and started talking *land reform*. Because the government owned all the actual land in Honduras, custom had allowed needful farmers to take over land not in use for worthwhile purposes. Now, however, the whole business began slowly to ferment like silage.

"These people want power," Don said. "Mel, did you see some of the signs in town the other day?"

"Uh-huh. *Yankee Go Home* and *This is Our land.*" Mel frowned. "I couldn't believe it. We've never seen anything like that before."

"I'm afraid we're going to have to reckon with this national movement before long."

In the midst of this foment, Ted and Joanne arrived, along with their busy toddler, Donnie. Ted quickly found plenty to do as work on the electric plant progressed. Waiting for the birth of their second baby, Joanne gladly helped wherever possible and organized her household. Twana offered the beige rug. "We've used it all these years, but it's still pretty good."

Ted, Tim, and Terry worked steadily alongside the ditch diggers. They took turns from dawn to dark with the recently acquired backhoe, scarcely allowing time off for meals. Twana constantly added plates at mealtimes as countless people arrived to help with the installation. Some stayed a few days. Others, like Hack and Mary Smith, special friends who helped with more than one project, remained longer.

During this time, anticipation of a new government added to the unrest throughout Honduras. "The fact that the former director of the Institute Nacional Agraria hasn't resigned yet helps keep the people stirred up," Don observed. "The best thing for us to do is just to lay low. Maybe after the inauguration of the new president this land reform business with the INA will more or less straighten up."

The morning of June 16, they knew the situation had not straightened up, but instead had knotted into an even bigger tangle. Campesinos invaded El Sembrador property.

"Well," Don exclaimed, "it looks like what we had hoped wouldn't happen is about to anyway. The campesinos want our land, whether or no. It's time for action."

Bumping over the rutty road on his way to Catacamas, Don watched the machete-wielding mob form a human barrier in front of him. *There they are. The campesinos have seen me coming, and it looks like they mean business.*

He scarcely knew he prayed as he shifted gears. Suddenly he yanked the steering wheel. The pickup swerved to the left and bounced off the road onto the field. Don slammed his right foot against the accelerator. The angry men could only wave their machetes impotently and turn to watch as he sped toward Catacamas.

Moments later at the meat packing plant, don Luis Oseguera immediately put his work aside. "Come on, Don. I'll go with you to Juti to see the lawyer and Colonel Padilla."

"We're glad the Colonel's in favor of the school. If anybody can help us he can. People listen to what he says."

Once Colonel Padilla heard the latest, he sent a telegram to the capital city, talked to military officials at Juticalpa, and dispatched fifteen soldiers and two officers. "They'll help control the invaders," he explained.

In the meantime, Don and the lawyer strategized, agreeing to make appointments with the president of Honduras, the Supreme Court, and with the Cattlemen's Association. "We can catch the noon plane out of Catacamas," Don suggested.

The plane had landed by the time Don and don Luis arrived back at Catacamas. "Is there any chance you can wait for me while I hurry out home to get my business papers and some clothes?" Don asked the pilot.

"Si, Señor Hawk," the pilot replied.

Wondering what he would find along the road to the farm, Don drove as fast as possible, relieved not to see campesinos waving their machetes. He pulled up in front of the Hawk house and ran inside to explain everything to Twana. They talked while she helped him toss an extra shirt or two and overnight necessities into a pockmarked cardboard box.

Twana kissed him and offered, "Ted and I'll drive you to the airstrip so we can bring the truck back out here."

No sign of trouble along the road this time, either, and as Don boarded the plane he urged, "Go ahead and continue planting where we've already started. I think the invaders have gone."

Ted remarked as he and Twana sauntered back to their vehicle, "It's good Dad's so tenacious when it comes to doing government business. He won't take 'no' for an answer."

"More than once he sat and waited rather than be turned away. He may have to do that again, or else back off and return another day. Your dad doesn't let fear get in his way when he needs to act. I'll never forget the evening a drunk man wandered onto the farm, waving a long machete and threatening to chop up someone. Don approached the man gently and talked him out of his murderous mood."

Now, with the noise of the plane almost drowning her words, she said, "He'll do what he has to this time, too."

Don returned home a few days later, too late for dinner with the family. Twana dished up leftover roast chicken and mashed potatoes and sat down across the table from her exhausted husband. "After you left," she told him, "our boys and the farm men drove the tractors in to finish planting like you said. Ted got there last, and just as he drove up the campesinos appeared out of somewhere."

"There's plenty of places for 'em to hide out there," Don muttered through the steam rising from his almost full coffee cup.

"Ted didn't have any weapons, but he managed to stop 'em from going onto the field while Tom raced back in the old Chevy to get help from the farm. In the meantime, though, the invaders apparently sensed something wrong because they disappeared again. The soldiers from Juti got there soon after, and to make a long story short, they were able to ferret out the invaders, surround and disarm them, and send 'em home."

Don cut another bite of chicken. "That's good news."

"We hear that the soldiers told them they were not to touch any more of El Sembrador's property. Also, I guess the campesinos were a pretty scared bunch since their leaders were in Teguc. The troublemakers out here couldn't understand how everything had moved so fast."

Don tipped the chair back onto two legs. "Well, so much for that. Of course it isn't all settled yet, but it's wonderful how the whole country seems to be coming to our defense."

Twana cut a piece of banana pie and started a fresh pot of coffee. "Through all this we're beginning to see who our real friends are."

"And aren't we thankful we have so many."

When missionaries in Tegucigalpa heard about the uncertainties at El Sembrador, they spoke their concern for the personnel's safety. "The campesinos mean business," they told each other.

On the morning of June 26, Don stood in front of the church. He watched while neighbors trooped to El Sembrador by foot from every direction. Trucks, rattly pickups, and bicycles ferried officials of various organizations, missionaries, members of the Catacamas and Juticalpa churches, and scores of others from the area.

His hands jammed deep into his pants pockets, Don prayed. *Thank You, Lord, that in spite of all our recent troubles the power plant's dedication is happening on schedule.* Even now he could still almost hear the high-spirited shouts that had signaled the first appearance of river water in the ditch. *We knew then it would be okay, praise the Lord.*

A dusty pickup rumbled past in low gear on its way to unload the folks standing like cordwood in the back. Don smiled and waved, then beckoned to Twana as she left the house. His face alight with excitement and anticipation, he reported, "I'm sure there are at least four hundred fifty people here."

Together they sauntered past the new pole on which someone had tacked a sign, handwritten in Spanish, *Jesus is the light of the world.* Many electrical lines fanned outward from the pole to the farm buildings.

Opening and closing prayers hemmed in the introductions and speeches that rounded out the day's program by the lake.

Representatives from the Honduran National Church, the Honduran government, the Cattlemen's Association, a bank official, Burnis Bushong of World Gospel Mission, and other *people of honor* spoke their appreciation for El Sembrador.

Don publicly recounted all that had happened to make this day possible. "We can never fully express our appreciation to many fine folks who had a part in this big undertaking. As you know, the Spanish word for light is *luz*. How fitting that the family who gave the money for this project should carry the name pronounced the same way but spelled L-u-c-e."

Missionaries began the applause that slowly built in intensity. "El Sembrador," Don continued after the clapping subsided, "would not be here today except for people like Mr. Joe Luce, president of the Blue Bird Body Company, who generously supports El Sembrador as did his father, A.L. Luce. We also thank hundreds of others who gave as they are able. God sent the right people at exactly the time we needed them for each part of this project, and the job was done with no injuries."

At last the sub-minister of natural resources pulled the switch. Immediately lights shone across the campus, looking wonderful even in daytime. Later, the guests ate the impressive barbecue dinner served under a large tree near the lake. They discussed the years that had passed so quickly.

"God has surely blessed this place."

"The farm has helped boys become useful men to the church and also to the country."

Work and stress-filled days followed the dedication as Don and Twana prepared for furlough. Talk of agrarian reform simmered along with a growing feeling of nationalism. "It's a problem other countries face these days too," said Don as he and Twana talked one evening long after everyone else in the house had headed off to their rooms.

"We need prayer now, maybe like we've never needed it before."

"Help from the Lord, that's the only answer." Don's muscular arms circled Twana. "Sometimes I wonder though if all these years of hard work and sweat will have been for nothing."

Twana replied slowly and softly, "Surely, oh Don...surely God won't let El Sembrador be taken over by the campesinos."

Don pulled her close, kissed her quickly, and released her. "Well, we pray not. Anyway, tomorrow's another day and if it's like I think it'll be, we won't have any spare time. We'd better get to bed and try to get some rest."

A few days later, Twana wrote in a letter to Jeannie, *The strain has been terrific, especially on your dad. Sure hope it clears up so we can leave on schedule.*

7

Ted and Joanne, along with all the Hawks, celebrated Jody Theodore's birth on July 9. As quickly as possible Don and Twana finished packing, said their goodbyes, and after confiding, "We're sure looking forward to this furlough, but to leave El Sembrador is like leaving home for a foreign country," drove down the lane.

"I feel good about Mel being in charge while we're gone," Don said.

They arrived at Washington Court House in time to help Jeannie with last minute preparations for her August 22 wedding to Dennis Johnson. After that, travels to churches where they told the El Sembrador story occupied their time. They readily informed friends and supporters about their family and the growing number of grandchildren that now included Cynthia Michelle, Tim and Sharon's April baby born in Bolivia.

All the while, thoughts of the farm and its boys stayed like indelible ink in the minds of Don and Twana. Only scanty information about the agrarian reform filtered north during their 16-month absence, and Don often said anxiously, "I sure hope INA will give back to us the land it took from our place there by Catacamas."

"The officials promised El Sembrador would get it back next year," Twana replied.

Don shook his head. "Somehow I don't feel much assurance."

On December 12, 1972, Don and Twana wrote a lengthy letter, detailing their overland trip from Ohio to El Sembrador with Tom Dunbar along to help drive. They ended by saying, *Thanksgiving day saw us nearing home and at 4:30 that after-noon we pulled through the gates of El Sembrador. We had spent many sleepless nights, loaded and unloaded the truck many times, started out as friends to each other and ended the trip as friends, saw many sights, met many wonderful people who helped all along the way, and truly God was with us all the way.*

We are now putting all the many things in their proper places, getting acquainted with our grandchildren, and we were present for the fourteenth graduation.

The next step is to get set up for the new school year that begins January 16.

Don and Twana saw Tracy off to boarding school once again, then began to learn the habits and whims of 140 boys. Knowing about the organized campaign started months before to discredit the farm school, Don said, "I'm sure our opposition has planted some boys here to disrupt things."

School personnel reexamined the secondary school, under way for some time, and concluded, "It doesn't seem to be hav-ing the results we want to see. Too many of the boys just want to come for the title and nothing else, and that's not our purpose."

Soon Don visited the education department in Tegucigalpa and asked permission to organize a vocational school, "which will help our boys most." Officials agreed, and that phase of the educational program commenced later.

Still, no settlement had come from the Instituto Nacional Agrario. "Although," Ted reminded his father, "INA has signed a document giving to the school the use of the land El Sembrador occupies."

"I just wish INA would hurry up and give us back the two hundred acres it took last year. We need them to make the farm more nearly self-supporting." With his customary big blue bandanna, Don wiped his forehead. "I wish, too, we had Dominio Pleno, but...well, maybe some day, Ted."

Granted only by the government, Dominio Pleno assured a farmer absolute title to the land he farmed. Thereafter, no one else had any right to it. Following 1973, until the time El Sembrador would receive the coveted favor, its advocates would unreel and sever tons of red tape and experience eons of anxieties.

Meanwhile, the accusations against the school gathered momentum like a truck headed downhill without brakes. Throughout February and March Tegucigalpa newspapers and the government, encouraged by the land reform movement, sent eleven commissions, one after another, to investigate El Sembrador.

Don reacted calmly. "We have nothing to worry about if only the commissions will give impartial reports."

Twana, weary with watching snoopy visitors lift lids off pans and taste food in the boys' kitchen, grumbled. "I suppose you're right. But if I see another commission heading this way I'd like to tell them to turn around and go back and just think what they want to think."

Rather than carry out her threat, Twana finally asked the commissions when they arrived, "Are you in favor of us or against us?" One man patted her on the back and replied, "Don't worry, doña Twana, everything's going to be all right."

March 1973

Dear friends,

It is Saturday afternoon and hot and dry. The bell rang a few minutes ago and the boys are getting their typhoid shots. Some don't mind them and others need a little persuasion.

We are surely grateful Hack and Mary Smith are here again. Hack keeps our machinery going and takes care of most of our maintenance. The garden Mary oversees is beginning to produce and will be a real boost to the kitchen. We are having the usual struggle to get some of the boys to eat their lettuce.

We are building two houses and getting ready to start on the vocational building. The light plant works on a 24-hour-a-day schedule that's wonderful.

The usual number of boys come and go for one reason or another. Some parents cooperate and some don't. Last night we organized the Young People's Group and almost half the boys want to take part in it. The enemy is working hard, and I will admit sometimes we get very low and discouraged, but then when we begin to count the many blessings God has given, we cannot help but rejoice.

Love and prayers,
Twana

The discrediting campaign kept going as unfavorable articles appeared in one of Tegucigalpa's major newspapers. When one article described the students as "being exploited and like helpless sheep living in a concentration camp," Saul Gómez, a friend of the school since its beginning, said, "I consider it my obligation as a Christian to say something."

In an article he later took to the newspaper's editor, Saul reiterated El Sembrador's purpose to *change lives and form boys into useful citizens.* He also reminded, *Escuela El Sembrador is an exemplary educational center supervised by the educational system of our government. ...a school like this developing and growing for twenty years and never receiving one penny from the government is not a business that is exploiting.*

He stated at the close, *If our estimation of Escuela El Sembrador is so far off, then name an investigation team that is honest and unbiased. And as a result of this investigation, if there are areas that need to be improved on, let them be improved...changed. We are in favor of that. However, we will not allow unjust accusations and injustice.*

Saul confronted the editor, who refused to print the article "until the school is closed and Señor Hawk has left the country." Saul talked fairness-in-reporting to the editor, who remained firm.

Someone said to don Saul, "If you offer money to one of these editors, he'll write a retraction."

"I'm not going to pay to have the truth printed. Besides, the article would be on a back page where almost no one would see it."

Saul took his cause to the other newspapers, showing the article he had written. Finally, the director at one paper asked, "Wouldn't it be better to have a report from the farm? To find out what's going on out there?"

"I can make the arrangements," Saul promised.

The director sent a reporter to the farm. Afterward the newspaper carried a center-spread article, complete with pictures and correct details that refuted everything reported in the original articles.

"It was a very nice article," said Saul during an interview in 1995. "I don't know who started it all, but no doubt someone paid the newspaper editor to write such negative information about the school."

After the new article appeared, parents of present and former Escuela El Sembrador students gathered in the Wright Memorial Church. To begin the meeting, someone read the newspaper article that made the strong accusations against the school and the principles it represented. Next, someone read the article written by Saul Gómez.

"Now," said Señor Suazo, the local educational supervisor, "we want your opinion. First, though, I will say there is a current that is trying to close the school by saying bad things about it. I have already, however, been in contact with the students, asking them if any of the accusations in the paper were true. None of them said anything against the school."

He turned to the El Sembrador personnel and said, "If there were any questionable areas in the accusations, be careful to take care of that right away. I do, however, congratulate you for a job well done."

Señor Suazo finished by admonishing the parents, "Unite yourselves."

One father stood to say, "I'm in agreement with you, señor."

Another rose to name all the benefits his child had received at El Sembrador. A third father stated, "My son has been at the school for six years, and he's been very happy there."

Two mothers expressed their thanks to the school directors for everything they had done for their boys.

José Acosta, a former student, awaited his turn to firmly avow, "Everything I know I owe to the school."

As the meeting concluded, parents who could write signed their names at the end of the two-page document, affirming their support of the school. Those who could not write signed with fingerprints.

Travis LaVerne, Ted and Joanne's third son, born on March 21, brought a new measure of cheer to his grandparents. Then, on April 26, they received the message that Twana's father had gone to heaven.

Don held Twana close and their tears mingled together as they prayed for themselves, for Twana's mother, and for all the family. They sat around the kitchen table to remember and talk, memories pouring out for recognition.

After a while Don said quietly, "I'll find out how soon we can get a flight out of Tegucigalpa."

After Mr. Baker's funeral, Twana informed her mother, "You remember that Terry's going to marry Colleen Lewton on June 1. Don and I have decided to stay until after the wedding."

Don traveled back to Honduras alone while Twana waited until the next month when she and her mother made the trip together. With Tracy home for summer vacation and Tom at El Sembrador briefly before his senior year in high school, Twana again enjoyed a semi-full Hawks' nest.

Late one afternoon Don returned home to say, "I've heard bad news. There's been a plane crash out at the Catacamas airstrip. One of the men just now drove in from town, and he told me he saw the plane. It's our Manuel that crashed."

Twana put her hands on Don's arms. "Oh my! I...I...'spose you mean Manuel Morales."

Don nodded.

"Was he...did...?"

"Yes. He was killed. And the three men with him too. Bank officials, I heard."

Don poured coffee, slurping the first gulp. "Apparently he came in for a landing, but there was a pig in the way. Manuel tried to miss it, but lost control of the plane and crashed—right into his sister's store across from the runway."

Her thoughts swept back to 1954 and she said, "Our little Manuel...in that first class...we didn't think he would really fly the airplanes he loved so much." She paused and then said, "It's always so hard to lose one of our boys."

The remaining months of that year crowded into one another as workers continued with improvements and additions to buildings. At the Cattle Exposition, El Sembrador won three trophies as well as other awards in the meat and milk classes. The soccer and basketball teams earned second place in both championship play-off games.

More than eighty boys, the annual report informed, *have come forward for prayer since the beginning of the school year. Spiritual progress is evident in many of their lives. Some of the boys go into nearby villages on evangelistic trips and also help in the services at the school.*

Don and Twana praised the Lord for exciting news from Dennis and Jeannie in September. "We received appointment with World Gospel Mission for service in Bolivia." A month later they announced the birth of their first son, Jason Scott.

With these family blessings bright as the Honduran sun at midday, Don and Twana could at last say, "It appears that the campaign against the school not only did not succeed, but that the government will guarantee the continued use of the land for the school. Although land taken last year has not been returned, it seems possible that it may be."

Hurricane Fifi struck the northern coast of Honduras on September 19, 1974. It changed the lives of many people, including those at El Sembrador.

1 9 7 4 — 1 9 9 3

1

Missionaries gathered for annual conference above Tegucigalpa at El Hatillo heard frightening radio reports. "One-hundred-forty-mile-per-hour winds...eight thousand dead...seventy-seven percent of the banana crop destroyed...."

"My goodness."

"Such destruction."

The missionaries prayed and afterward wondered aloud, "What can we as a mission do to help up north?"

Someone suggested, "How about a committee to investigate the damage and find out what's needed?"

Agreement brought action, and Ted soon encouraged, "By all means, Mom and Dad, I think you should head up the relief work. We'll gladly double up at the farm." Others nodded and Tom Dunbar, who directed World Gospel Mission's work in Honduras, affirmed, "After all, that's a needy project."

"Would you look at that," Don exclaimed, as he and Twana first viewed the devastation. "The mountainside sluffed off as if it was nothing. My, oh, my! Trees and rocks everywhere. And sand and water."

"Oh, Don.... Where can we even begin to help? It looks hopeless. These people lost everything. Crops. Homes. Absolutely everything."

They listened to heartbreaking stories of entire families washed away, of parents who struggled helplessly as their boys and girls slid out of reach, of mothers drowning while their children watched.

"These folks want a helping hand, not a handout," said Don as they planned their tactics.

He and Twana settled into a small house in Feisitranh (FACIE-trahn), a suburb of San Pedro Sula, sharing the residents' after-storm isolation. Until workers could rebuild the bridge between this colony and the city, only the hardy dared ford the out-of-control river. Those first few weeks the Hawks both gave assistance and received it. Hurricane survivors shared their skimpy food supplies with Don and Twana and helped haul away more than thirty truckloads of sand, logs, and trash from Hawks' yard.

Don organized work teams to clear yards and houses still standing but full of water and debris. He and Twana led nightly services in their home and three meetings each Sunday. A graduate of El Sembrador and several Bible school students from the capital city came to help.

God has blessed in a wonderful way, Twana wrote. *We have seen many souls won to Christ and much interest in the gospel.*

Each day, Twana stayed in Feisitranh to help pack beans, rice, salt, sugar, corn, flour, and meat for one hundred homes. Don concentrated his work in Quebrada Seca (KwayBRAHdah SAYkuh), a village whose name meant *Dry Creek.* There, boulders as big as houses had leveled everything when they plunged down the mountains during the storm's frenzy.

"We'll help you locate to a safer place," Don told the displaced residents. With funds from World Gospel Mission, World Relief Commission, and the Churches of Christ in Christian Union, he purchased land. "Each family will work a hundred days in order to receive a house," Don explained. "We'll give you food but we can't pay wages."

His energy stretched to match the days of slow travel to the village eight miles away followed by oversight of the work. Professional masons and carpenters, hired with donated funds, did the building. Local men cleared land, hauled materials, laid foundations, and made cement blocks while women carried on their heads the five-gallon cans of water dipped from mountain springs.

"I don't think I could ever describe all that's involved in this work," Don said one evening. "There's so much red tape for this and that. It's sure a long process."

After living at Feisitranh for two months, Don and Twana moved back to El Sembrador. They heard how the Talgua river, swollen with heavy rains, had ripped apart its usual boundaries. "The backlash from the hurricane," Ted said. "It was really hard on our crops. And our light plant, too. After lightning hit, it worked at only half capacity 'til we got it fixed."

Don maintained a strenuous pace, up at four in the morning and busy continuously until well past dark. More and more others heard him say, "I'm just too tired to deal with that tonight."

They shook their heads and asked, "Is Don working too hard?" Some even remarked, "He's not his usual jolly self."

Still, he and Twana headed north for a few days now and then to oversee the reconstruction.

Dedication for the first fifty-seven houses at Feisitranh took place on March 15, 1975. Families gratefully received their new sturdily built homes, ample yards, and outside toilets built of cement blocks. They organized a cooperative business and a store. Work continued on twenty more houses, a church, a home for the pastor, and a clinic. A graduate of El Sembrador served as pastor to the congregation that filled the church every service.

The colonists announced, surprising Don and Twana, "We have named our new settlement *Colonia Twana*." They also gave them a large carved Seal of Honduras.

In October, Catherine Jean, soon nicknamed Kitty, arrived as the first daughter in Ted and Joanne's family. El Sembrador missionaries remarked about the year's high spiritual tone. Farm workers calculated Hurricane Fifi's damage to the farm school fields and reported, "The crop loss here wasn't as serious as in other areas of the country."

The 1975 school year opened with 121 students. Don declared, "This will be the final year of the secondary agricultural course. We feel that vocational training would be more practical for the boys."

Tim Hawk, assisted by Redys Romero, a former El Sembrador student with vocational training, taught industrial arts classes to interested students. This program, which included carpentry, masonry, and toy-making, remained unofficial until January 1976 when the vocational school opened for classes in the new building. Along with the original studies, the school offered instruction in furniture making, upholstery, and various types of wood art.

At 3:04 the morning of February 4, Twana jerked upright in bed. "What's that noise?"

Don rolled over and mumbled, "I don't know."

"It sounds like a truck right here in the house. The house is shaking, and the dogs are barking too. I'll see what's going on."

Twana padded down the hall to the living room, then into the kitchen. A hasty look onto the dark yard gave no answers. She opened the screen door but still saw nothing unusual. *Oh, well, whatever it was must be gone now.* She sighed and crawled back into bed to sleep until the usual getting-up time.

Just before noon, the radio snapped into life, demanding attention. Twana signed on, listened, talked, listened, then said, "I'll tell him," and concluded the transmission.

She rushed outside, nearly colliding with Rolando as he rounded the corner lugging a huge stalk of bananas. "Have you seen don Donaldo?" Twana inquired.

"Si, doña Twana. Over there by the barn. Shall I put these bananas on the porch?"

"Si. Gracias." Twana hurried toward the barn, calling, "Don! Don! I have a message for you."

He showed up in the door with shovel in hand. "What's up?"

"I just talked to Tom Dunbar on the radio, and he said that noise and shaking this morning was an earthquake in Guatemala. He asked if you would go up there for World Relief Commission to find out how much damage the earthquake did. Then you could make recommendations about relief work. He said he's heard that up to three hundred people were killed."

Don leaned against his shovel while they briefly discussed the ins and outs of Tom's suggestion. Deciding he should go, they started back to the house. "Tim and the others can handle things here," Don said.

"This quake obviously wasn't as strong as the one that hit Nicaragua in 1973."

"We sure knew when that one hit. I remember it cracked a wall in our house."

Little time passed before Don boarded a missionary plane and headed west into Guatemala. "The news usually exaggerates the damage in a situation like this," he told the pilot. "It probably won't be as bad as we've heard it is."

By the time he finished meeting with missionaries and Guatemalans and after he saw the damage firsthand, Don reported, "The estimates were not exaggerated. In fact, it's a whole lot worse than anyone thought."

Two days after the earthquake he headed back to Tegucigalpa. He had no more than arrived when he heard, "Another hard quake has hit Guatemala with even more disastrous effects."

Don, along with Tom Dunbar, traveled back to Guatemala in the following weeks to oversee World Relief Commission's efforts. After they finished and returned home again, Don spoke to the schoolboys gathered in the church.

"They're saying now that more than seventeen thousand people died in that earthquake, and they find more bodies all the time. Boys, in just three years a major disaster has hit three different countries next to each other. Earthquakes in Nicaragua and Guatemala and the hurricane here in Honduras. Each time, within a few seconds, thousands of people died. They didn't have time to pray or get right with God."

He cleared his throat and looked at the rows of faces, light caramel all the way to dark chocolate. "Those of us here, now, had better keep prayed up and doing our best to win others to Christ."

More than sixty El Sembrador schoolboys took the suggestion seriously, and at the end of the message they walked forward to kneel at the front to give their lives to Christ.

June 1976

Dear friends,

This month the senior Hawks will fly north to start a year of furlough. We will leave the farm school in good hands with Tim and Sharon having charge of the overall aspect of the work. Don and Eunice Coffman and David and Lavena Bushong will be coworkers with them.

The spiritual aspect is very good and healthful. Boys are taking great interest in outside evangelism as well as with their own classmates.

Though the land taken from the school several years ago has not been returned, there has been no further land invasion, and government agencies have given a verbal guarantee that El Sembrador will not be affected by additional invasions.

> *Sincerely in Him,*
> *Don and Twana Hawk*

Rolando Alvarez graduated from El Sembrador primary school that year and then enrolled in the new vocational school.

In January, twenty-two boys, El Sembrador primary school graduates, began their training in woodcarving, cabinetmaking, and general carpentry. Sales proved brisk for items the boys made. "We're not able to keep up with all the requests we get," said Redys Romero.

One student studied farm machinery maintenance and operation along with welding. Later, Dave Bushong, the son of Burnis and Thelma Bushong and an accomplished photographer, offered instruction in photography.

When Don and Twana returned to Honduras that October, David Tracy stayed to continue high school in the States. Non-family members now knew him as *David*. Earlier, when school personnel placed *Tracy Hawk* in the girls' dorm, he had made a quick decision.

Grandchildren pictures readily offered for viewing showed Dennis and Jeannie's sons, Jason Scott Johnson and his younger brother, Aaron Chad. The album also included Timothy Shannon, son of Tim and Sharon, and Jeremy Andrew, the first baby for Terry and Colleen, beginning their missionary service at World Gospel Mission's Southwest Indian School in Arizona.

Away from the constant pressure, Don had relaxed. He and Twana felt ready to face new challenges. "Even though Don will be the crisis coordinator for World Relief Commission," they stated, "he will still be the executive director for El Sembrador."

They moved to Tegucigalpa and settled into the World Relief Commission house at 1810 8th Calle, a narrow street with houses close on both sides. Don traveled to Central and South American countries, assessing the need for aid after natural disasters, while Twana maintained her role as hostess. Later, she accompanied Don around the world on behalf of World Relief Commission.

They undertook the new assignments with mixed feelings while admitting, "We hope to have many contacts with El Sembrador graduates."

Don saw Roque Caranza downtown in Tegucigalpa one day. After greetings and hugs, Roque said, "Mi amigo, I'm so glad to see you. You must come to visit Josie and me again soon."

"How's everything going at Valley of the Angels?" Don asked.

"We're very busy, señor, with many children at the orphanage now. We do everything just like I learned at El Sembrador." Roque's face crinkled with good humor. "We even hide Easter eggs." Then he added seriously, "God used you and doña Twana to prepare me for my future ministry."

One evening at home after supper Don sat in a large dark mahogany rocking chair. "You know, Twana, it thrills me that no matter where I travel in Honduras young men come up and remind me that they were students at El Sembrador."

Don took his glasses off, pulled out a blue bandanna and wiped the black-framed lens. "They all tell me how grateful they are for the privilege of attending El Sembrador. Most of 'em say, 'I learned to work at El Sembrador, even if I didn't want to.'"

He shoved the handkerchief into a pocket and slid his glasses into place. "That's why so many people want to hire our graduates. They know how to work."

"Well, it's all because of what God has done, not what we've done."

Missing daily life at El Sembrador, Don and Twana drove out to the farm whenever time allowed. Once, Don took a package into the Catacamas post office where the postmistress greeted him with enthusiasm. "Hola, Señor Hawk. We are always happy to see you. I want to tell you about my nephew that went to El Sembrador." She straightened her shoulders and proudly explained, "He has just graduated from Harvard University in your country. That's because of your school."

By 1978, El Sembrador's records listed three hundred graduates, approximately ten times that many having attended. Zoa Lemus, a careful statistician, pointed out to Don, "Twenty-five percent of our Honduran National Church pastors graduated from El Sembrador. Besides, many of the men now in the government agriculture department went to school here."

"We can't thank God enough for the way He's answered prayer," Don replied.

Zoa closed the record book and said, "Another dental team'll be here next week."

"Yes. In fact, Twana's going out to the villages to help."

Regular visits from volunteer dentists had significantly improved the local dental health. Sometimes they saw patients on the front porch of the main house at El Sembrador, and other times the teams set up makeshift dental facilities under village trees. Grateful Hondurans patiently lined up to wait their turns as they listened to Bible stories, gospel songs, and invitations to receive Christ as their Savior.

When Tim and Sharon left for furlough in June 1978, Don Coffman agreed to become the farm director. "I suppose you heard," he told Don and Twana, "that David Castro and his wife, Ela, are coming back to work with us here at the farm."

Twana giggled. "Remember how we laughed when we heard David wanted to have their honeymoon at El Sembrador? I didn't know if Ela would agree to that or not, but she did."

The Castro family moved to the farm before school opened that year. David counseled the schoolboys and also directed the evangelism program, training students to witness in nearby San Luis, La Paz, San Pedro, and Rio Tinto. Eventually these villages as well as others developed organized congregations as a result of this program.

Even before this time, Ela battled the problems of an improperly functioning heart valve. "Whenever you come into Tegucigalpa for your doctor appointments be sure to make our home your headquarters," Don and Twana urged.

The Hawks planned their schedule to include the annual Day of the School celebration, held each year on July 19, Don's birthday. They relished the games, races, barbecue, dramas, and general merriment as much as the boys did.

Watching the boys line up for the three-legged race, Twana asked Don, "Did you notice how slow Ela walks now?"

"Yes, and her color isn't good either. I'm afraid she's getting worse, not better."

David and Ela continued the endless visits to the doctors in Tegucigalpa during 1979 and 1980. Before 1981 progressed beyond the first quarter, David told Don and Twana, "The doctors tell us there's nothing they can do for Ela here in Honduras. They say she'll have to go to the States or to Mexico for the surgery she needs. We know that will cost a lot of money."

Don gripped David's shoulder. "Now don't be overly burdened about this. With your faith, God will open doors."

Early in July, telephone conversations between Don Hawk and Don Coffman on furlough in Iowa nudged that door. At last Don Coffman reported, "Finally we've got everything arranged for Ela's surgery. Doctor Muellen from Milwaukee, Wisconsin, has agreed to do the surgery."

"I knew God would work it out."

"But wait, there's more," said Don Coffman. "Doctor Muellen says he'll see that everything's cared for financially, either by the hospital or through his church."

When Don Hawk saw David and Ela again, he told them, "I have your tickets. You both will fly to the States on Monday the twenty-seventh."

"But...but don Donaldo, I don't have money to go with her."

"I realize that, David, but I've taught you boys to be men. We must act. Everything's going to be okay. God has provided. I'm going out to Olancho for a few days, but I'll be here to take you to the airport."

Monday, July 27, Don and Twana told David and Ela goodbye, and Don hugged both of them three times. As the Castros headed into the airport departure area, Don called, "Ela, when you get back, I want to see you run, and David, we have to get a Bible school started at El Sembrador."

Twenty-four hours later, Ela rested in the Wisconsin hospital. Tests would occupy her time the next day. "That'll be a good time for Eunice and me to take David to visit the World Gospel Misson office at Marion, Indiana," Don suggested. "We'll get back here in plenty of time for Ela's surgery next week."

Seeing them approach the World Gospel Mission headquarters building, David Bushong, by that time a staff person there, opened the large glass front doors. "Let's sit down over here," he said quietly. He led the way to the chapel area and pulled four chairs into a tight circle.

They sat down. David Bushong inhaled deeply and said, "We need to pray, but first I must tell you that God has taken don Donaldo to be with Him."

2

In the dining room at 1810 8th Calle on Tuesday morning, Don Hawk finished his breakfast coffee and sighed. "I don't know why I've been so tired this weekend, but I guess I better get up and at it. Lots to do today." He pushed back from the table. "I'm sure anxious to hear how everything's going with David and Ela in Wisconsin."

"I suppose someone will let us know before long." Twana carried dirty dishes from the table to the kitchen.

"I'll probably be gone most of the morning. While Tom's still here with us he needs to see the dentist, so I'll drop him off for that appointment and then go on up to the hospital for my checkup. After that I've got some business to tend to."

Don kissed Twana goodbye, and under a sun still pleasantly warm he and Tom drove out of the driveway.

Downtown, Don stopped briefly to let Tom out at the dentist's office, then pulled back into heavy traffic. Minutes later he swung the car into a lot, parked, and started walking the four blocks up the hill to the hospital.

He crossed the street and passed the pharmacy at the corner half a block from the hospital. A few more paces and suddenly his toe caught in a hole. Don lurched forward and grabbed uselessly at the roughly plastered wall alongside. He sprawled face down on the dusty sidewalk, remaining motionless.

Two men veered around Don and hurried on their way. Several others stopped long enough to look more closely.

"He's probably drunk," a well-dressed woman suggested before she crossed the street.

Inside the pharmacy, a young woman gasped. "I know him. That's Señor Donaldo Hawk. Quick. Someone get help." She ran outside and knelt beside Don. *Thieves will steal his valuables. I can't let that happen.* She removed Don's billfold and watch. Sometime later she returned them to Twana.

Meanwhile, Twana sat at her desk composing a letter. *There's so much I want to tell our supporters, more than one page can hold, I'm sure.*

The raucous sound of the telephone uprooted her thoughts. The words she heard stole her breath. "Yes, I'll come right away."

She made another call immediately. "Elladean, Don's at the hospital downtown. They say he's had a heart attack."

The only WGM missionary in town at the time, Elladean Harrell quickly promised, "I'll come right now and take you to the hospital."

The dense late-morning traffic moved at turtle-speed along the narrow downtown streets. Drivers honked impatiently, vehicles clogged the intersections. "There's no place to park anywhere near the hospital," Elladean lamented.

"Just let me out in front."

Twana dashed into the hospital. Someone guided her to the emergency room where Don lay stretched full length, face up, on the high, flat, narrow gurney. Twana quickly recognized the truth.

"Don!" she cried. "You're too young to die. You're too young..." A sob choked off the words as she placed her warm hands over his, now limp and unresponsive.

Elladean entered noiselessly and put her arm around Twana, no words needed. Another missionary friend tiptoed in, followed by Billy Harrell, World Gospel Mission field director, who had rushed down from El Hatillo. Others joined them as the news spread.

"Don is dead? Oh my."

"I...I'm sorry... I didn't know. All I heard was that he had a heart attack."

They all searched for comforting words to offer Twana and each other, as well.

Billy whispered to Elladean, "I'll go intercept Tom before he gets here. Don's secretary called him, but he doesn't know his dad is dead."

Tom, however, did not stop to hear what Billy wanted to say. Instead, he burst into the group. "Dad...? Mom? What's...?"

"He's gone, Tom," Twana explained quietly. "He had a heart attack."

Everyone turned from their own shock to surround Tom, suddenly pale and speechless.

The rest of the family received the news quickly. A radio message to El Sembrador notified Tim and Sharon. Dennis and Twana Jean in Bolivia heard via phone. Another call alerted Terry in Washington Court House, and he told Ted and Tracy, working nearby.

Before long, coherent thoughts shaped into plans.

"Twana?" Billy asked. "Do you want to have a service at the farm?"

"I...I think so, don't you, Tom?"

He nodded his agreement.

A few telephone calls later he said, "Mom and I'll fly out to Catacamas by MAF plane late this afternoon. The mortician will take Dad's body in the hearse and then bring it back for a service here in town tomorrow morning."

Tim and Sharon stood in the farmhouse kitchen looking at each other. Everything else had suddenly gone out of focus.

"Dad gone?"

"That's hard to believe. He was just here last week."

Both minds unwound memories faster than words could organize. Here in this room Dad poured hundreds of cups of coffee. How many times had he knelt to pray beside the chairs spread around the table? How many measures of discipline did he hand out to his children as they faced one another here? Had anyone ever recorded the number of wrestling matches between Hawk sons and their father on this floor? Who could count the times Dad kissed Mom goodbye here in the kitchen? Hondurans by the dozens came for counsel or prayer or encouragement and sat with Dad on these chairs while he took time for them.

Finally, words formed from Tim's thoughts. "Just last Friday he and I spent the day out at La Mosquitia."

"He wasn't himself though," said Sharon. "He was almost grouchy, and that wasn't like him."

"But he roughhoused with the kids and hugged everybody goodbye before he left."

With one arm around Tammy and the other circling Cindy and Shannon, Tim said, "We'll all miss Grandpa."

"I know," sobbed Tammy. "He won't be here to play checkers with me."

"Or to tease us anymore."

Sharon's face relaxed, smoothing out the frown. "I want to play the piano for the service tonight. I know Zoa always plays, but I want to this time."

"That's a good idea. Dad liked to hear you play."

The news sailed around the area as swiftly as a jungle bird fleeing an enemy. Farm workers, teachers, volunteers, school-boys, and neighbors filled the house and yard, offering sympathy and help.

"We'll need to get a lot of food ready," some of the women projected.

"The farm workers are butchering chickens today. Let's fry up a bunch of those."

Before long the women had a mound of drumsticks, backs, breasts, and thighs floured and into the fry pan. Two monstrous pans of sliced potatoes drowned in rich white sauce sat ready for the oven when the three chocolate cakes finished baking. Several big bowls of grated cabbage, fragrant with vinegar and spices, waited on shelves inside the walk-in cooler.

Dora, wife of Joche, one of the first workers at El Sembrador, and whose sons had attended school there, stood outside the Hawk front door. When Sharon called out, "Come in," Dora rushed inside and threw her arms around Sharon. She continued sobbing before she could assemble her voice. "I can't believe don Donaldo's gone. He always came to our house and sat at our table and drank coffee." She cleared her throat and wiped her eyes. "And if it wasn't for him we wouldn't have the water system in our village."

At the church, teachers and others swept then decorated it with green leafy plants from staff homes and colored paper flowers pinned to the walls. They braided pastel crepe paper ropes and draped them over several front pews where the family would sit.

A few minutes before six o'clock, Tim drove the farm pickup to meet Twana and Tom at the Catacamas airstrip. By the time they returned to the farm, the schoolboys, wearing their navy blue pants and light blue shirts, lined the road on both sides. No one laughed, made loud remarks, or pushed the one standing next. A few shyly waved.

Twana walked directly into the house to sit in the living room for the coming hours. Doña Chocha, her longtime friend from Catacamas, sat quietly beside her.

One by one or in groups small and large, people walked or drove to El Sembrador, some from nearby, others from far away. Hearing the piano music in the church, they stepped in slowly to sit and weep or kneel at the altar. In the Honduran custom, these friends and neighbors felt free to speak their words of honor and respect for Don. Some moved silently from the church to the house to shed tears with Twana.

When the mortician arrived, hours later than anyone had anticipated, Tim said, "Mom, it's time for us to go over to the church."

Hundreds of mourners crowded onto benches, stood along the wall, or watched from outside as Twana and her family took their seats, a sign for the service to begin. Arcides Lemus read Scripture and then prayed before Tammy and Cindy sang "Lejos de mi Salvador," one of Don's favorites. When the girls finished, Arcides stood tall and straight to speak comforting words, and then ask, "Would anyone else like to say something?"

From all sides of the packed church people stood, taking turns to speak of don Donaldo, who over the years had become one of them. They looked up to him for reasons far beyond the fact that he had come to them from North America. This man of sterling character had earned their respect and appreciation.

A singing group from Tegucigalpa interspersed their songs between the affirmations. At last, near one o'clock Wednesday morning, Arcides asked once more, "Does anybody else want to say something?"

Luis Oseguera, who had stayed all evening, rose slowly. With tear-filled emotion uncommon to Honduran men, he said, "I remember Don. He considered our friendship as something special, and he was never too good for our cattlemen's parties; he came even though we all knew he didn't drink."

He shifted his feet and continued. "He always asked me, 'When are you going to become a Christian?' Tonight..." Luis swallowed several times before he finished the sentence. "Tonight I want to say, don Donaldo, it's not goodbye, it's *until later.* I expect to see you in heaven."

Paper flowers near open windows quivered in the slight breeze. Night insects flitted from one light to another, while far away a cow mooed anxiously in the dark.

Tim walked to the platform to face the damp-eyed crowd. "It's a sad time," he said, "but inside it's a happy time because we know that someday we'll see Jesus. We're proud that Dad touched so many lives."

Twana, Tim, and Tom flew back to Tegucigalpa at day-break. Others drove, arriving in time for the nine o'clock service at the Honduran Holiness Central Church.

Government officials, businessmen, missionaries representing many organizations, World Relief personnel, and dozens of people unrecognized by Twana filled the church. When Manuel Figueroa stood to speak, Twana's mind reeled back to 1948 when he visited their home regularly. *I knew Manuel would make something of himself.* With a graduate degree in microbiology from an American university and as a university professor, he had become one of the most influential Christians in Honduras.

"The path of a good man is prospered by the Lord," Manuel said. "I felt a great admiration for Don. We're sorry he's gone, but still we feel it is a triumph for a life well grounded."

Sounds of children, busy in their school classrooms at the other side of the church, blended with music and spoken words to honor the life of Donald Hawk, known and respected throughout Honduras. Denominational leaders had considered dismissing the day-school classes during the service, but decided, "No, school will go on as usual," someone suggested. "Life with the children was Don's life, so it's fitting for us to listen to their voices in the background as we conduct the service."

In the short time since Don's fall to the sidewalk, many people had helped make final arrangements for transporting Don's body to Ohio. Wednesday afternoon a customs agent met Twana and the other five Hawks at the airport. "We can't believe it," he said.

An attendant in the parking lot looked at Twana with tear-filled eyes. Another young man, who always sold a newspaper to Don, quietly watched the Hawks then turned away. "He didn't know what to say," Tim whispered to Twana. "He knows Dad cared about him."

All of Honduras grieved that day, which government officials had decreed a "Special Day of Recognition" for the man who had not just *felt* sorry about needs, but who had unsparingly *done* something about them.

Familiar, comforting music wrapped around Twana as Ted seated her on the front pew of the Heritage Memorial Church, the old Gregg Street Church with a new location and name. Hawk sons, daughter, daughters-in-law, and grandchildren arranged themselves beside and behind her.

She took a deep breath. The previous three days stood out like a well-painted picture, framed with love and encouragement. Cards, food, flowers, and other gifts had streamed into Ted and Joanne's home.

In the sweet bye and bye...we shall meet on that beautiful shore.

As the prelude music concluded, Dr. Stan Toler, Heritage Memorial pastor, stepped behind the pulpit. He waited a moment as ushers searched in vain for additional seating for latecomers.

"Let's bow our heads for prayer. Our Father and our God, how grateful we are this afternoon that we can approach Thy throne of grace and know that You provided for us in times just like these. We ask, our Father...."

After prayer, Tracy sang "It Is Well with My Soul," followed by more music that praised God and spoke of the heavenly home. Representatives from World Gospel Mission, World Relief Commission, family members, and others expressed remembrances.

"Don's probably the only man who would start around the world with a cardboard box and a paper bag. He didn't spend a lot of time worrying about the job or getting ready; he just went out there and did it."

"...we had to have a man of compassion. Don was that kind of man. He had tender hands, but hands willing to become soiled with the reality refugees faced."

"Dear Dad," said the letter written by Twana Jean and read aloud by Ted. "...You were such a mixture of kindness, courage, love, honesty, energy, hard work, fun, laughter, seriousness, dedication, generosity, tenderheartedness, and faith. We will sorely miss you."

Burnis Bushong recounted his first meeting with Don Hawk. "I didn't know at that time I was meeting a man who would become a legend."

Another reminded, "Hondurans live and eat better because of Don Hawk. Descendants of his full-blooded cattle, horses, pigs, and chickens have improved the quality of livestock throughout the nation. And out in Olancho, Don pioneered the cultivation of hybrid corn. Honduran markets in the area are now filled with green vegetables not available before Don introduced them."

"El Sembrador stands as a memorial to what God can do through a man."

Dr. Toler introduced David Castro, "representing the church in Honduras."

"I am a part of the fruit of Donald Hawk," David said. "The people knew him in the street, in the marketplaces, in the towns, in the kitchens. He identified with the people."

"*...Because He lives, I can face tomorrow...Because I know He holds the future...*"

After the last song, a final prayer, and condolences from friends, Twana and her family walked slowly out of the church, the first steps into the future.

3

Home again at the farm in mid-November 1982, Twana stood under the large guanacaste tree in the front yard. Animal noises and people sounds signaled a happy welcome to this busy place. Memories washed over her like gentle rain.

El Sembrador. The Sower. And now Don's gone to be with the Sower Himself. But his dreams live on. He worked hard to improve the quality of life here. Ours was the first tractor in Olancho and later our combine was the first in all of Honduras. And Don's modern farming techniques were something Hondurans hadn't seen before.

Three big blue-black birds sporting long tails took their space in the tree overhead. A handful of tiny brown birds, twice as big as dandelion fluff made themselves nearly invisible under a bush. *There's no place quite like it. Even after all these years I still love the flowers and birds, though civilization has sent a lot of 'em farther into the jungle. Most of the wild animals are gone, too, so the boys don't hunt like they used to.*

Two energetic boys waved and yelled, "Hola, doña Twana." *The boys. There are so many now, we don't give them the five pieces of candy every Saturday. But it's the boys that make El Sembrador special, different from other farms—boys like Miguel and Juan and Santos and Roberto and Hector.*

Dormant memories quickly returned as flesh and blood. *Hector. Hector Newman from La Ceiba on the north coast. He came by plane into Catacamas. His first flight, and I remember how sick he was by the time the plane landed. Then later on he loved to help me with Tracy. Hector took him outside to play or watched him when Don and I went to town. I remember he told us, "I like to practice the few words of English I know."*

And David Castro. Another wonderful boy God sent to us. Don would feel so pleased to know Ela is well now and that someone else took care of all her surgery and hospital expenses.

Immersed in the atmosphere, fragrant with the scent of limonario blooms, Twana inventoried the last sixteen months since Don's death. First the hurried trip to the States and back to Honduras so Jeannie could help sort and pack. Later, months in Ohio for rest before fund-raising and the return to the farm.

Everything about the farm looks the same, yet everything looks different without Don here. The new dining room and kitchen. What a blessing. Headquarters sure organized the construction team in a hurry after the fire last year.

Strolling toward the church, Twana's thoughts accumulated news she wished she could share with Don. *More missionaries here now, even Terry and Colleen who transferred from Southwest Indian School... Francisco Castro will take over as farm director when Tim and Sharon move to Tegucigalpa next month... I felt so happy and proud when the National Congress declared you "an exemplary citizen" and the motion passed to a commission to prepare it for law... I'd like to show you the plaque from the National Association of Evangelicals commemorating your work and also the "Distinguished Service as a Missionary" plaque given to me from the Churches of Christ in Christian Union...*

Twana opened the wide front door and leisurely walked to her usual place halfway up on the right side. She sat down. *One thing was always clear. God called us to Honduras. And right now, it's just as clear, God has called me to Honduras. I feel as if I fit right here, like stepping into an old shoe.*

In the next three years, Twana grew accustomed to life without Don. She kept wiggly boys interested in Sunday school for forty-five minutes each Sunday morning on her porch. The dining room sometimes turned into a teaching room as she oversaw the ambitious boys through three meals every day. She supervised the kitchen, driving the compact station wagon into Catacamas to buy supplies at the market. Her wise calculations kept ample amounts of garden produce, milk, meat, and poultry from the farm on hand every day.

Women's groups, committees, and visitors took time and attention. After one particularly busy season, Twana calculated she had served two thousand guest meals.

Don Hawk's dream of a Bible school at the farm turned into reality with David Castro as the director. The El Sembrador staff decided to honor Don, changing the farm school's official name to Escuela El Sembrador Donald Hawk. Enrollment reached 176.

The family grew to include more grandchildren. David Tracy married Deborah Mayo, and a few months later they chose to help at El Sembrador. Twana had a bout with physical problems. In 1986 she wrote, *I have battled diabetes and am winning, more or less....*

Later that year, September 23, surprising news arrived via radio. *The wife of the president of Honduras will visit El Sembrador tomorrow.*

Immediately everyone moved into high gear.

Eunice Coffman mobilized a group of boys and marched them toward the dump to cut weeds with their machetes. Another missionary gathered boys to clean the church, then later they decorated it with fresh flowers. Others swept the sidewalks and tidied the classrooms. "Be sure your dorm rooms are clean," someone else admonished.

Zoa directed a hasty rehearsal of the National Hymn. Teachers organized a program, selecting several boys to recite poems. Twana, with other women assisting, planned a meal for the visitors.

Early the next morning the security detail arrived in cars and motorcycles, and the men stationed themselves in strategic places. The schoolboys, dressed in their light blue shirts and darker blue pants, lined up after breakfast to watch for the first lady of Honduras. At last the advance guard arrived on his motorcycle to make the initial security check.

Soon the official motorcade brought Señora Mirian de Azcona with her entourage of five women and more security guards. After greetings, missionaries escorted doña Azcona, gracious and smiling, wearing a white skirt and variegated pink knit top, and her friends on a tour of the dairy barns and classrooms.

Their walk ended in the church where excited students presented their hastily rehearsed program. Afterward the visitors filed into the Hawk house dining room Twana and her helpers had decorated with vases of flowers on white, embroidered tablecloths.

As the guests finished the meal, cooked American style from food grown and produced at El Sembrador, the president's wife talked about the social service program she directed for needy children. "Some of the boys from my program have come here to school, and I can't believe the big change in them. I wanted to come and see for myself what has made the difference. How many psychologists do you have at El Sembrador?"

The missionaries looked at each other.

"None," one replied.

"Jesus Christ is our greatest counselor," one teacher said.

Another offered, "It isn't us, it's God who makes the changes in the boys."

A member of Señora Azcona's party suggested to her, "We need more schools like El Sembrador."

"Yes," she replied, "but that would be difficult. These people work because of love."

One evening the next week, several missionaries sat at ease around the big table in Twana's dining room. Coffee and cake accompanied the business discussion. "The floor in our church sure is getting bad," someone mentioned.

"It's the tiles. They're terribly uneven."

"I wonder if we should consider building a new church. We've used this one for twenty-seven years."

"We could get by, I suppose, by just repairing the floor."

They made no decisions that evening. Heavy rains, however, soaked the area that week, and on Sunday afternoon everyone knew a new building must rise in place of crumbled walls. With the moisture that crept up the west wall from the bottom and down from the top, the adobe bricks reverted to the original soft clay. Some caved away to the outside, others fell inside onto benches.

"I'm sure glad these walls didn't give way while we were in here for service this morning," Twana said, as the farm residents surveyed the damage.

"At least the roof held," Eunice noted.

For the next eighteen months, volunteers from the States grouped into work teams under the leadership of Terry Hawk, the new farm director, to construct the new adobe brick church. Twana carried out her normal furlough schedule in the States, arriving back at El Sembrador in time for the dedication of the David Guest Memorial Chapel, named in honor of a special friend.

Visitors and friends admired the striking three-tiered tower above the entrance, the red-tiled roof, and the white walls. Spacious and airy with high cathedral ceilings, the sanctuary had space for almost five hundred people. Woodworkers at the vocational school crafted from dark Honduras mahogany the handsome altar rail, new benches, doors, window frames, and other furniture.

Exactly one week after the dedication, a windstorm of hurricane strength ripped off portions of the roof. A fresh call for volunteers brought additional workers to repair the damage.

Finished the second time, the new church commanded Twana's attention. *God made it possible. What a fitting memorial to David Guest and to Don, also. And to Zoa. I sure do miss her.*

One morning several weeks before, a schoolboy knocked at the Hawk's front door with an urgent message. "Doña Colleen, you're needed at the Lemus house."

Moments later everyone knew, "Doña Zoila is very sick."

The next message stunned all who heard. "Zoa died a few minutes ago."

Teachers immediately dismissed school. Plans for Zoa's service blossomed quickly. Boys hurried to clear away construction leftovers and move the benches back inside the unfinished church. Women decorated with traditional paper flower wreaths, lavender, white, and pink, arranged among large green plants.

Later that same day, hundreds of people drove, rode, or walked to El Sembrador for her service. Many spoke of the "greatness of this special lady." Vilma Castro, a teacher alongside Zoa at El Sembrador, said, "I've never seen a better school administrator."

"Her life was lived for Honduras and her people, but especially for her boys at El Sembrador," said another.

Arcides received permission from government authorities to bury his wife alongside the east wall of the church. Later, a special stone placed there and engraved with *Vivo para Servir* forever reminds that Zoa *lived to serve*.

Now, with thoughts of Zoa's smile and her constant, competent helpfulness, Twana faced the new church. *I don't know how we could have developed the farm school without her.*

As the decade of the '80s ended, Twana noted the list of missionaries at El Sembrador. *Twenty-one adults, with two more preparing to come. Oh, how Don and I prayed for such abundant help. And with a Honduran director of the Bible Institute and classes in the new primary school building now and the new metal trades shop, I can see real progress. I'm glad workers remodeled the old classroom building into apartments, mine included.*

Behind the chapel, four big greenhouses, constructed from metal frames, plastic covers, and netting, stood ready to take their place in the farm's daily life and livelihood. *I'm thankful God sent Larry and Angie Overholt to us. He's got wonderful plans for the greenhouses, and with Angie as the nurse... Oh, how I used to wish we had a nurse here.*

Even as Twana mentally outlined the progress, she knew local campesinos still caused trouble. *Seems like there's always something to try the farm director's patience. Even so, Lord willing, the farm will soon be deficit free.*

4

The seasons, dry and wet, signaled the passing of time until 1991, the year Twana reached the age World Gospel Mission missionaries must retire. The mission officially recognized her retirement at the annual Celebration, forty-four years after she and Don had received their first public introduction to WGM supporters.

"But since we have the privilege of continuing year by year," she explained to family and friends, "I plan to return to Honduras."

This she did, but not until she had fully recovered from the February 1993 heart by-pass surgery.

Meanwhile, at El Sembrador, troubles poured out like beans from a torn sack. Thieves tried more than once to steal cattle from the farm. Campesinos asked the National Agrarian Institute for permission to invade El Sembrador property. Don Coffman, the farm director, received the notice that squatters intended to take part of El Sembrador's land.

Right away, the institute, informally called INA, sent an agronomist to make a formal study. "They have to see if El Sembrador has full rights to the land or if we have to turn it over to the squatters," said Don.

A collective sigh of relief rose from El Sembrador when the agronomist reported, "Squatters have absolutely no right to invade the school's land." Under the law, the farm school had lived up to its obligations.

The squatters reapplied. INA sent another agronomist to make a second report. At the same time, the local radio station allowed squatters to inject threatening speeches into daily programming. "Come down and negotiate with us," they urged.

"It's not our place to negotiate what's already ours," said Larry Overholt.

In the midst of the anxiety, prolonged by the squatters, who had the right to apply as many times as they wished, Don and Eunice Coffman left for a short medical leave to the States. Larry took over as interim farm director.

One morning, Arcides arrived at the greenhouse with the news, "The squatters have invaded our property again. Ten families, and they want four hundred and thirty acres, all the way from the Talgua River to the Guayape."

"And they've probably got good support behind them," Larry replied.

By now nearly seventy years old, Arcides rearranged his big straw hat and muttered, "Yes, but we can't let them have our land."

The roots of this new harassment had begun to take hold a few days before when a tall Honduran said to Larry, "We're from the high school in Catacamas."

A shorter, younger man added, "We want to borrow a dump truck from your farm."

Standing beside the umbrella-like banyon tree near the main farmhouse, Larry replied, "I'm sorry, but the truck isn't available now. It isn't working, and we can't fix it because there aren't parts anywhere here in Honduras. Come back when we have the parts, and we'll talk about it then."

Almost instantly, locals used that conversation to promote an extensive propaganda attack against El Sembrador. A few days later, the Honduran Labor Day holiday, Catacamas high school students went on strike. They joined with the campesinos to discredit El Sembrador.

Members of this new alliance railed loudly in speeches at community holiday festivities. "El Sembrador was uncooperative. They wouldn't loan their equipment when we asked."

Others chimed in to say, "The school is rich. It doesn't need that much land."

With that background and now this fresh news, Larry told Arcides, "I should call Don and Eunice in the States and let them know. They can alert our friends there about this urgent prayer request."

Trouble rode a seesaw the next few weeks. The squatters left almost as abruptly as they had come, then appeared again nearly as quickly. The Coffmans returned to El Sembrador as that all happened.

Don and Larry leaned against the blue Ford tractor under overhanging branches of the huge, old Palo Verde tree that gave welcome shade from the hot morning sun. Don's dog, Lucy, gray and white with black ears, flopped down and set her left hind leg in motion to scratch an itch behind that ear. "Don Hawk wouldn't have backed down in the face of this discouragement," Don stated. "We can't back down either."

Before day's end, Don talked with the missionaries and the Honduran staff. "Don't just stand by," the nationals urged. "Do something."

"The only way I can fight it is through the legal process," Don replied. "I'm not like some who take other means to fight a situation like this."

First, he called the school's lawyer, Gumercindo Escobar, in Tegucigalpa. "This is the first I've heard about this invasion," Gumercindo answered. "I'm upset to think they'd try it again. I'll be willing to do anything to protect the school. You know, if it wasn't for the school, I wouldn't be what I am today."

"Let's meet in Juticalpa tomorrow and go to the INA office together," Don suggested. "If anybody can help, the people there can."

Next, Don headed into Catacamas to talk to the congresswoman from that district after someone reminded him, "Under our government she has quite a bit of power. Besides, she had two cousins who went to El Sembrador. One of them, you remember, later went to the States and graduated from Harvard."

The congresswoman, however, had gone to Tegucigalpa. "Congress is in session," her husband said, handing her phone number to Don.

When Don spoke to the congresswoman on the phone, she replied, "I'll do anything I can to help you. What time will you go to the INA office tomorrow?"

"About eleven o'clock."

The next day, Don and the president of the Catacamas Cattlemen's Association met Gumercindo at the INA office. The conversation did not start off well, and only after the congresswoman called the INA director, did Don feel certain of his help. Later Don said, "I've never seen a man's attitude change so fast. Something she said made him an instant friend of El Sembrador."

The rest of the day Don and Gumercindo spent time and traveled miles to gain more support. Military men and government officials pledged their help. "Thank the Lord for the contacts Don Hawk made during all those years," Don said. "God put these men in the right place at the right time."

The local radio station continued to broadcast in favor of the campesinos, while national radio and newspapers also picked up the cause. A phone call alerted mission headquarters in Marion, Indiana, about this crucial need for prayer.

A few days later, the Congress announced that a team of investigators would soon visit Olancho farmers whose land had been invaded. Besides government officials, this team would include campesino representatives, one from the national level and one from the local campesino union.

Don told Eunice one morning, "I don't know what time this commission will come today, but I halfway expect them to be here for dinner."

"I'll ask Angie to help, and we'll have dinner ready," Eunice promised.

The visiting team drove onto El Sembrador property late that morning. Don showed them around the farm and school. As they started to leave, a Honduran invited, "Come on down to where the squatters are."

Overhearing the conversation, a Honduran teacher's wife ran to the main house, straight into the kitchen. "Doña Eunice, they're wanting our men to go down where the squatters are, but the missionaries shouldn't go with them. It's too dangerous. Don't you have dinner ready?"

"Yes."

"Then I'm going out to tell them they must come in and eat."

She dashed back outside and shouted, "Dinner's ready and it'll be ruined if you don't come and eat it right now."

The men offered no resistance.

Once inside, missionaries and visitors sat together at the long tables in the dining room. Eunice and Angie served the roast beef and mashed potato dinner, refilling the bowls of tangy farm-grown cabbage salad and pouring cup after cup of strong, hot coffee. Fresh rolls quickly disappeared from two napkin-lined baskets.

Seven-year-old Maria Overholt observed the careful attention the women gave the commission men. She whispered to her daddy, "Are these men kings or something?"

Larry smiled at his daughter and looked around the table. *This is an interesting situation,* he thought. *Here we are sitting down with people who've invaded our property and who want to take it away from us.* He shook his head in disbelief and buttered another hot roll.

The man at his left, a member of the campesino union, jabbed his fork into the last two bites of meat on his plate. "You know, it's interesting. When we were coming out from Catacamas my plan was to do everything within my power to take as much of the school's land as we could. You're just a school, and I didn't figure you needed that much land. My people need land, so I thought we would leave you with just the school and that was about it."

Angie offered a piece of chocolate cake as the representative explained, "I don't know what happened, and I can't understand it." He frowned and shook his head as if he walked through cobwebs. "When we turned into the lane out here, my attitude changed. I realized our people are wrong. We shouldn't be on this land. I'm going to recommend that our people leave the school's property."

A few days later, the squatters picked up their belongings and left.

"We know why those people changed their minds," said Larry.   "We sure do," Don replied. "It's because people prayed and God answered."

Later, the missionaries verbally pieced together their patches of thoughts about the miracle. When they had finished, the pattern of what should come next became clear.

"I think now's the time we should heed the suggestion of the minister of natural resources," said Don. "He says he'll do all he can to help us get our Dominio Pleno. That's the only way we can stop these invasions."

Endless travel, sleepless nights, and myriad consultations lay between that day and November 16, 1993, when Terry Hawk would receive from President Rafael Callajas (CahYEAHus) the important document granting Dominio Pleno to El Sembrador.

"Before you can fill out all the papers, you'll need the exact measurement of all the land El Sembrador uses," said Virgilio Barahone Lagos, an engineer and a staunch friend of the school since his student days.

"Will you be able to do that job for us?" Don Coffman asked.

"Si, señor. I will gladly help our school."

It took several months to complete the painstaking job. After Virgilio accurately measured the land and calculated placement of buildings, he visited dozens of offices in the capital city to make sure he had completed the requirements. For all this work he charged only a minimal fee.

Later, engineers from the States said, "We could not have done the details in the minute way he did."

"I feel honored and happy that you chose me for this job," Virgilio told the missionaries. "If I had not come here to school I could never be what I am today. Perhaps I would not even be alive. Everything I have I owe to God."

Many days Don Coffman left home early and returned late at night as he made the rounds to get important information. He visited all the landowners whose land joined El Sembrador. Their signatures indicated agreement with the stated farm boundaries.

"How much will we have to pay the government for the land?" Don inquired. When he had the answer, he told Larry, "If we pay what they want, it could amount to sixty thousand dollars. I'd better see if we can negotiate that price."

The minister of natural resources heard Don's request, and suggested, "You write a letter to the national director of INA. Make a copy for President Callejas and one for me, too. Have it here by seven o'clock tomorrow morning and I'll hand deliver it to the president."

With the help of other missionaries, Don wrote the letter that night, offering the government less than one-third of the asking price. The minister presented the letter to the president, and two weeks later reported, "He has accepted your offer."

The message containing the date of the public ceremony at which El Sembrador would receive Dominio Pleno did not reach the farm until Tuesday morning, November 15. Judy Crist, head teacher for El Sembrador's Missionary Kids Academy, heard the news on her way to her classroom.

"Are you willing to dismiss school for the day so the kids can go into Juticalpa to see Terry receive the Dominio Pleno papers? We're going to take the schoolboys, too."

Judy laughed. "It's a good thing *flexibility* is our motto. Of course we'll dismiss."

Less than an hour later, two busloads of El Sembrador residents headed for Juticalpa. By the time they arrived at the city square, hordes of people had already started to gather. A platform stood at one end of the park. Blue and white banners with President Callejas's picture and name on them flapped from wires strung overhead. Blue balloons, decorated with the Nationalist party's insignia, swung back and forth under the roof that protected the platform from the fiery sun.

"Let's stand here," said Terry Hawk. "It's close to the platform so I can easily get to the front when it's El Sembrador's turn."

Time passed slowly and the temperature soared as everyone waited for sight of the president. When information circulated, "Today's his birthday," attention shifted to the special table at one side of the platform.

"Look," Colleen said to Terry. "That cake on the tiered stand must be a birthday cake. See, it's in the shape of the presidential palace in Tegucigalpa. That's cute the way they've decorated it with a Honduras flag and a sign with his name."

Terry squinted as the sun reflected like a thousand watt bulb in a window across the street. "When President Callejas was secretary of agriculture he came out to Olancho every now and then. I remember Dad telling me how he'd visit the government agriculture school and then come over to El Sembrador. He was really impressed with our farm and school."

Turning away from the reflection, Terry said, "I sure appreciate all he and his government did to help us get Dominio Pleno."

At the sound of the helicopter, faces turned upward. "That's him," several people shouted. A few minutes later, President Callejas, wearing an open-necked light blue shirt and gray pants, arrived by car.

He smiled and waved and readily shook hands with those he met as he walked from the car to the platform. The onlookers, nearly ten thousand people from all over Olancho, pushed closer together than ever. Sweat poured down faces and seeped through shirts and blouses. Young children fretted and fidgeted or leaned damply against adult legs and shoulders.

On the program first, several city officials announced government-working-with-city projects to benefit many people. President Callejas stood to speak next. He inaugurated the new Juticalpa water system and publicly recognized the group from El Sembrador.

He spoke of other matters important to the area and then at last, presidential aides called one-by-one the names of those to receive the coveted papers bearing their land titles. Recipients walked in front of the platform, shook hands with the president, then stepped away with relieved sighs and pleased expressions.

Finally an aide said, "Terry Hawk, representing Escuela El Sembrador Donald Hawk."

President Callejas smiled and motioned Terry onto the platform. "It gives me much pleasure to be able to present the title of *Dominio Pleno* to such a deserving institution. Your school has made an important contribution to Honduran society. You've made it possible for thousands of boys to have an education, preparing them for a better future. You have proved that a school can survive without government support, and everyone can see how well the school is accepted, how the community respects it. El Sembrador holds values other than knowledge that are important for the region and for the country. You promote strong moral values, a work ethic, and a will to serve the community. With very few resources, you are able to generate such good results."

He handed Terry the paper conferring clear title to El Sembrador's 1,800 acres, gripped the missionary's hand, and shook it heartily.

Terry returned to his place alongside the others from El Sembrador. The oppressive heat no longer mattered. Weariness faded away like shadows exposed to sunlight.

The missionaries beamed. *Truly we found favor and good understanding in the sight of God and man.*

ALBUM

1. Donald and Twana Hawk after her high school graduation

2. Don and Twana, Teddy and Timmy, before going to Honduras

3. The original house after Don and Ellery Echlin built the fence (1948)

4. A good place to get lost—only a few yards from the house (1948)

5. Wooden kegs slung over the horse's back brought water from the river.

6. Remodeling the Hawks' house (1952-1953)

7. North and west sides of the house (1959)

8. A handy laundry center under the bell that kept everyone on schedule

9. Manuel Morales, a member of the first class, who later fulfilled his dream of becoming a pilot

10. First school dorm with an addition

11. An early graduating class with the dorm in the left background

12. The Hawk family (1962) right to left: Ted, Tim, Jeannie, Tom, Terry, Tracy

13. 1970: Tim, Sharon, Tom, Terry, Joanne, Ted and Donnie, Tracy, Twana, Don, Twana Jean

14. Arcides Lemus

15. Hurricane devastation in north Honduras (1974)

16. A new colonia develops after the hurricane (1974)

17. The Wright Memorial Chapel, completed in 1959

18. West side of the chapel after the cave-in (1985)

19. The president's wife visits El Sembrador in 1985. Twana helps
    serve dinner to her.
20. David Guest Memorial Chapel

21. A view from the chapel platform

22. Arcides and Zoa Lemus in later years

23. Hungry boys with their rice and beans
24. 1989 graduating class
25. Sign at the entrance to El Sembrador
26. Present day primary school building

25

26

27. From one small plow and disk to a shed full of modern farm equipment and buses

28. Terry Hawk (right) waiting to receive Dominio Pleno papers from President Callejas (1993)

29. Eager boys waiting for a share of an abundant harvest (1995)

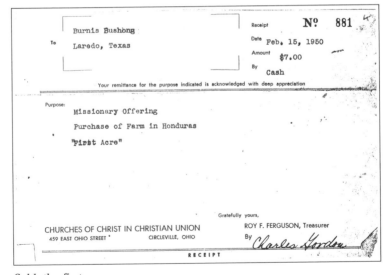

Sold: the first acre

30. New boys dorm, finished in 1995

31. New dining hall with the original bell

32. Greenhouse operation supplies plants for El Sembrador and the community.

33. Installed in 1995, the water tower preceded a new water system for El Sembrador.

34. Long-legged members of El Sembrador's herd

35. Granaries located between the farm buildings and the road now provide adequate storage.

FINALLY...

1

"You don't realize what you have there," the son of one of the richest men in Honduras told a WGM missionary soon after Dominio Pleno day. "Our family has a farm in northern Honduras. We have tried to get Dominio Pleno for thirty years and haven't been able to." Another attested to the fact that his group had tried for thirteen years.

The timing of that day became a miracle in itself. With national elections scheduled twelve days later, the missionaries knew they might have to start the process to secure Dominio Pleno all over again. "That's what often happens with a change of government officials," Terry explained to a visitor. "Anything that's already been done or money already spent isn't recognized as valid anymore. But thank the Lord He helped us finish everything in time."

2

The remarkable blessing of *absolute title* brought an end to some troubles, but did not restore to El Sembrador acreage the campesinos had taken years before. Hopes rise that perhaps that will happen even yet.

Other complications and accusations, however, wait in readiness to break out at unexpected times. Loyal friends of the farm school speak out on its behalf when necessary.

With Don Hawk's vision for a self-supporting farm now a reality under Terry's able leadership, crop production remains a primary concern. Teacher's salaries, school materials, and food depend upon it. A variety of marketable crops from the fields and the greenhouses, along with income from selling milk and beef cattle, provide needed cash. El Sembrador receives cash when its workers operate the farm equipment on a work-for-hire basis for nearby ranchers. Financial appeals directed to El Sembrador friends in the States raise money for special projects not covered by the school budget.

Students still organize early morning prayer meetings, and their outreach continues through preaching and Christian education. Enrollment stays near two hundred, and as from the beginning, the school meets all the Honduras education requirements. Applications for entrance now come from many well-off families, and missionaries sometimes find it difficult to decide which boys to accept. "We don't want to turn away the really needy students," they say.

One old dorm makes way for a new one, and a separate clinic building eases the task for the school nurse, Angie Overholt. A Christian Honduran doctor regularly comes to help Angie. Lillian, a nurse who grew up in nearby La Paz where she gave her life to God as a result of El Sembrador's outreach, assumes the medical work while Angie goes on furlough.

New farm equipment gradually replaces old, worn-out machines. With special permission from the Honduran government, these enter the country duty-free.

Vocational schools at El Sembrador teach young men how to support themselves through woodworking, auto mechanics, agronomy, and horticulture. A well-equipped machine shop adds another dimension to their education. Young women students at the Bible school learn sewing skills.

More than four thousand boys and young men have received spiritual and academic training at El Sembrador. Many of them stand out in professional and vocational circles.

3

In cooperation with the Honduran Holiness church in Catacamas and the local community, El Sembrador began a new phase of education at the beginning of the 1996 school year. Buildings on donated land between the farm and town will eventually house the new day school, El Sembrador-Horeb Technical High School. In the meantime, the students attend classes in the El Sembrador facilities. This long-planned addition gives junior high and high school youth another opportunity for quality education in a Christian atmosphere.

4

Missionaries sponsored the first-ever El Sembrador alumni reunion in November 1996. About one hundred former students returned to the farm, many for the first time since leaving school years ago.

"We must see all the farm," they said, curious about the changes. A new water storage tower, the lake and power plant many times larger than they had known years ago, the new water and sewage systems, four large greenhouses, tall lights that lined the big athletic field west of the church—these obvious changes along with those less noticeable brought nods and words of approval.

"All these improvements happened," said Larry, "because many people prayed, gave money, and came down here to do the work. We thank the Lord for these friends. We could not have done it without them."

In the evenings, the alumni sat on the farmhouse porch. Recollections passed back and forth as fast as the soccer balls they had kicked with youthful surefootedness. Their laughter drifted over the farm like the sweet fragrance of flowers Twana planted long ago.

Tim Hawk led four special services in a large tent assembled on the athletic field. Discussions included instructions to help the men become responsible husbands and fathers, as well as how to take spiritual leadership in the home. Many made spiritual commitments, some for the first time.

"The seed of God was planted in my heart when I was a student here," one man testified. "The seed hasn't grown, but it hasn't died yet, either."

Not long after the reunion, the missionaries noticed radical changes in two experienced El Sembrador farm workers, also former students, and their wives. Even the schoolboys wondered what had happened.

"We have decided to follow the Lord," the two men explained.

They began to witness in nearby villages. Soon, their home village, El Carbon, near El Sembrador's lake, experienced a spiritual revival. The Sunday night these workers gave their testimonies to the schoolboys, the altar hardly had room for all who knelt to pray. Later, several sought out staff members to say, "Please forgive me for my behavior."

5

Arcides Lemus, dear to everyone at El Sembrador and also to many who visited through the years, suffered a stroke in mid-1997. He slowly improved, and ultimately returned to his home at El Sembrador. Never completely gaining a full measure of health, Arcides requires house help twenty-four hours a day.

Missionaries and other friends recall the strong, confident, and wise farm worker of past decades. His consistent support and that of Zoa as well, helped form the framework of El Sembrador. "They more than carried their share of responsibilities," says Twana. "We can't overestimate their importance to the farm school."

Joche Hernandez, who as a ten-year-old accepted Don Hawk's invitation to work at the farm and then later joined the first class, worked at El Sembrador until his retirement in 1995. His sons attended El Sembrador and stayed on to work, also.

Jorge Pinto never forgot all he learned at El Sembrador. At last he left his wayward ways, returning to God's plan for his life. He pastors a growing Honduran Holiness Church in Tegucigulpa

Hector Newman finished the primary grades at the farm, and later moved with his family to Boston, Massachusetts. He finished high school there, received a college degree, and later a master's degree before studying toward a doctorate. He became a United States citizen. In 1980 with his wife and children, Hector returned to Honduras as a church planter, supported by his denomination, Conservative Baptist. "I'm the first Honduran our church has sent to Honduras as a missionary," he says. "But at El Sembrador I got established in my Christian life."

Rolando Alvarez (Hawk), married and with a family, lives at El Sembrador and directs the woodcarving department at the vocational school.

David Castro pastored for many years the large Honduran Holiness Church in Catacamas. In early 1998, the denomination elected David to serve as president for a three-year term. His wife, Ela, assumed pastoral duties at the Catacamas church.

New missionaries at El Sembrador take over where others left off. Volunteers continue to come in steady numbers.

Will a third generation of Hawks someday serve the Lord at El Sembrador? The possibility appears certain, in God's timing.

6

C harles Barton, the teenager who lived with Don and Twana in the mid-1940s, continues to reside in Washington Court House. He married, had a family, and as time passed, took leadership roles in a local church. Charles retired from his vocation in industry.

7

Confident in the Lord's leading, Don and Twana determined to follow Him *come what may.* "Don was the leader," a friend observed, "but Twana backed him all the way. She was a 'woman of iron.'"

Now, with the passing of time, others carry on.

Twana lives most of the year in her Washington Court House home, a commodious house skillfully remodeled by Ted, Tim, and Terry. Great delight comes when the Hawk family gathers at her home. She attends grandchildrens' weddings and graduations whether far or near.

As often as possible, she spends several months at El Sembrador.

Twana always remembers names and faces of former students, no matter where she meets them. Upon hearing of their successes, she rejoices. When discovering some do not live up to the spiritual challenges they received in school, she continues to pray for them.

Her heart and mind will never stray far from El Sembrador, come what may.

Twana Jean Baker Hawk...

...a wife and mother of noble character.

She is worth far more than rubies.

Her husband had full confidence in her...

she brought him good, not harm.

She worked with eager hands, getting up while it was still dark;

she provided food for her family, ample portions for her house helpers and abundance for undernourished schoolboys.

She set about her work vigorously; her arms were strong for her tasks.

She opened her arms to the poor and extended her hands to the needy.

Her husband was respected at the city gate when he took his seat among the elders of the land.

She is clothed with strength and dignity; she can laugh at the days to come and smile at the days now passed.

She speaks with wisdom and faithful instruction is on her tongue.

She watched over the affairs of her household and did not eat the bread of idleness.

Her children arise and call her blessed;

her husband did also, and he praised her.

(Based on Proverbs 30, New International Version)

On February 25, 2000, Twana joined Don in heaven.

Portions of the letter written by Twana Jean Johnson and read at Don's memorial service in Ohio.

August 1, 1982

Dear Dad,

These past few days have seemed so unreal. It is still hard to grasp that you have gone. And yet, as I look around I see you have left so much of yourself behind. I see so much of you in my brothers' big hands and full stature so like yours, certain facial features, posture, walk, and talk. I see you in their mannerisms—one has your directness, one your total honesty, another your gentleness, your generosity, courtesy, love of God, and love of people. We are all composites of what you were. We are all so different and yet because of you and Mom, we are so alike. Your love for us kept us close to each other even though for so much of our lives we have been separated by miles. You were such a mixture of kindness, courage, love, honesty, energy, hard work, fun, laughter, seriousness, dedication, generosity, tenderheartedness, and faith. We will sorely miss you.

We don't remember you teaching us principles and virtues of life verbally, but we learned by the example you set before us. Your influence did not stop at home. Everywhere we turn people are telling us how much you meant to them. "There was never a better friend." "He cared so much for people," and on and on. You may have been just a farmer with no long degrees behind your name, but you didn't need them. Why? Because you let God take what you had and He made great things happen through you. In doing this you showed us that no matter what happened, the most important thing in life is to do what we feel is right in God's sight. Then all the other blessings fall into place.

Your accomplishments will be lauded by others. For us, it was enough to have you as our father. You instilled that pride in us because you were proud of us. In this day of divorce and trial relationships you and Mother also taught us a fierce loyalty and love for our mates. By your example again, we learned that love is given and kept through joys and trials. Trials only seemed to bring you two closer. There was no doubt of your love for each other. You have left us quite an inheritance.

Farewell—

THE HAWK FAMILY TREE

Donald Frederick Hawk   m.   Twana Jean Baker

---

1. Donald Theodore (9-7-44)   m.   Joanne Watkins
   (Former missionaries, World Gospel Mission:
   El Sembrador; business; and nursing)

   Donald Harold (12-28-69)   m.   Holly Mills
       Don Travis   (1-28-95)
       Skyler Samson (6-6-96)
       Wendy Gale   (9-14-97)

   Jody Theodore (7-9-71)   m.   Mitzi Koch

   Travis LaVerne (3-21-73)   m.   Lori Sturgill

   Catherine (Kitty) Jean   m.   Matthew Taylor
      (10-30-74)

   Angela Marie (1-13-82)

2. Timothy Neal (12-6-46)   m.   Sharon Davidson
   (Former missionaries, World Gospel Mission: Bolivia,
   El Sembrador, homeland staff)

   Tamra Jean (1-3-71)   m.   Kevin Miller

Cynthia Michelle (4-21-72)   m.   Brian Carey
   Joshua Caleb (1-30-95)
   Alexis Nichole (3-11-96)

Timothy Shannon (11-30-76)

3. Twana Jean (11-7-49)   m.   Dennis Johnson
(Missionaries, World Gospel Mission: Bolivia; Bolivia
Field Director; WGM Latin American Coordinator

   Jason Scott (10-30-73)   m.   Nicola Yssel

   Aaron Chad (12-21-75)

   Nathan Matthew (11-13-77) m.   Stephanie Mayer

   Jeannie (7-9-82) stillborn

   Twana Joy (6-13-85)

   Denise Happiness (6-13-85)

4. Terry (1-3-53)   m.   Colleen Lewton
(Missionaries, World Gospel Mission: Southwest Indian
School, El Sembrador)

   Jeremy Andrew (5-19-77)

   Benjamin Ryan (11-20-82)

   Jennifer Ann Marie (12-14-84)

5. Thomas Ray (6-3-56)   m.   Sharon Lister
   (USAID San Salvador, El Salvador)

   Courtney (6-14-80)

   Ryan (6-28-85)

                                    m.   Claude Dumont Alvarez

   Ariane Sibone Dumont (4-10-72)

   Julio Funes Dumont (2-28-78)

   Diego Funes Dumont (8-15-80)

6. David Tracy (3-4-60)   m.   Deborah Mayo
   (Missionaries, World Gospel Mission: Texas/Mexico
   border, Honduras)

   Blake Anthony (5-11-86)

   Taylor Adam (1-14-93)

   Kaitlin Nichole (12-21-95)